IN A LANDSCAPE

IN A LANDSCAPE

ↁↄ

POETRY BY

JOHN GALLAHER

AMERICAN POETS CONTINUUM SERIES, NO. 146

BOA EDITIONS, LTD. ↁↄ ROCHESTER, NY ↁↄ 2014

First Edition
14 15 16 17   7 6 5 4 3 2 1

For information about permission to reuse any material from this book please contact The Permissions Company at www.permissionscompany.com or e-mail permdude@eclipse.net.

Publications by BOA Editions, Ltd.—a not-for-profit corporation under section 501 (c) (3) of the United States Internal Revenue Code—are made possible with funds from a variety of sources, including public funds from the New York State Council on the Arts, a state agency; the Literature Program of the National Endowment for the Arts; the County of Monroe, NY; the Lannan Foundation for support of the Lannan Translations Selection Series; the Mary S. Mulligan Charitable Trust; the Rochester Area Community Foundation; the Arts & CulturalCouncil for Greater Rochester; the Steeple-Jack Fund; the Ames-Amzalak Memorial Trust in memory of Henry Ames, Semon Amzalak and Dan Amzalak; and contributions from many individuals nationwide. See Colophon on page 128 for special individual acknowledgments.

Cover Design: Sandy Knight
Interior Design and Composition: Richard Foerster
BOA Logo: Mirko

Library of Congress Cataloging-in-Publication Data

Gallaher, John, 1965–
[Poems. Selections]
In a landscape / John Gallaher. — First edition.
    pages cm
   ISBN 978-1-938160-50-9 — ISBN 978-1-938160-50-9 (ebook)
I. Title.
PS3607.A415A6 2014
811'.6—dc23

                                    2014011179

BOA Editions, Ltd.
250 North Goodman Street, Suite 306
Rochester, NY 14607
www.boaeditions.org
A. Poulin, Jr., Founder (1938–1996)

Now   for a moment   let's consider   what are the   im-
portant questions   and what is that   greater earnestness
that is required.

—John Cage, *SILENCE*

They are the same aren't they,
The presumed landscape and the dream of home
—John Ashbery, "The Bungalows"

CONTENTS

IN A LANDSCAPE

I

"Are you happy?" That's a good place to start, or maybe,
"Do you think you're happy?" with its more negative
tone. Sometimes you're walking, sometimes falling. That's part
of the problem too, but not all of the problem. Flowers out the window
or on the windowsill, and so someone brought flowers.
We spend a long time interested in which way the car would
best go in the driveway. Is that the beginning of an answer?
Some way to say who we are?

Well, it brings us up to now, at any rate, as the limitations
of structure, which is the way we need for it to be. Invent some muses
and invoke them, or save them for the yard, some animus
to get us going. And what was it Michael said yesterday? That
the committee to do all these good things has an agenda to do all these
other things as well, that we decide are less good in our estimation,
so then we have this difficulty. It just gets to you sometimes. We have
a table of red apples and a table of green apples, and someone asks you
about apples, but that's too general, you think, as you've made
several distinctions to get to this place of two tables, two colors.
How can that be an answer to anything? Or we can play the forgetting game,
how, for twenty years, my mother would answer for her forgetfulness
by saying it was Old-Timer's Disease, until she forgot that too.

On the television, a truck passes left to right, in stereo. Outside,
a garbage truck passes right to left. They intersect. And so the world continues
around two corners. The table gets turned over, with several people
standing around seemingly not sure of what comes next. Look at them
politely as you can, they're beginners too. And they say the right question
is far more difficult to get to than the right answer. It sounds good,
anyway, in the way other people's lives are a form of distance, something
you can look at, like landscape, until your own starts to look that way
as well. Looking back at the alternatives, we never had children
or we had more children. And what were their names? As the living room parts
into halls and ridges, where we spend the afternoon imagining a plant,
a filing cabinet or two . . . because some of these questions
you have with others, and some you have only with yourself.

II

"Ghosts are people who think they're ghosts,"
my daughter Natalie said, starting off the period
we will refer to later as A Little Bit Further Along. Since then
(which was last night, November 3rd, 2009), I've been thinking
about where I am more, as a kind of goal,
and somewhat less about where I'm not. It's a pleasure to be
where one is, given that someone
isn't somewhere lethal. This is Pleasure One.

And now this is Pleasure Two, thinking about it,
so that this place, which was Place One, and a pleasure,
as we were there where we were and it was not a lethal place,
but a place where we were, is now this place again
as we're here thinking about it, like America or a Popsicle.
"Open the house and the house is empty," Natalie also said, meaning
her dollhouse, as she's seven, but when she said it, I had this
vision of all of us suddenly disappearing, maybe thinking
ourselves ghosts, even, or getting somewhere, out
and around her bedroom and then down the hall and stairs.

I'll tell you how it happened. Natalie and I were looking out the window
at the backyard, and she asked me if I liked our house. It's a theme
with her. The other night she asked me if I liked life. I said, "Yeah,
a lot." And she looked at me a second and then said, "Me too."
You don't hear that every day, I think, until the accumulations
begin to remind me of every day: Carla, who donated a kidney
to her brother-in-law (Robin's uncle), has just been diagnosed
with cancer, two months later. She sends hopeful updates
from the hospital, on Facebook. Like fountains, the footnotes
go on. My footnote or yours. The big questions can't be decided
in this way. They demand coins or laws. And this is
much too important to be a big question.

III

It appears that we're living (which isn't always the case), depending
on how one defines such things, in a "Now you see it /
now you see it" kind of way. We can say we're working on our age,
as well, listening to Bob Dylan songs where people can age
in whatever direction supports the theme. "Too bad life doesn't
get themes," Robin says, and yes, that's right, and then we can all go
do whatever it was we were going to do anyway. "It's either that,
or pay off the kidnapper," as Neil Young had it, back in the mid-70s.
There's always an analogue, and someone to tell us about it,
how, no matter how fast you run, you can't run fast enough
to get away from yourself. You could even call it a theme.

For instance, I was the first one to an eighteen-wheeler accident
on the highway once, in the early 90s. I didn't know what
I was going to find. It was just tossed there on its side, across
both lanes. So I got out of the car and walked around to the front,
only to see the driver standing inside the cab that was resting
on the driver-side door. He was simply standing there behind the glass,
parallel with the dashboard, a little blood on his forehead, looking
as lost as I felt, looking back at him. All his things (magazines
and maps and cigarettes and pens and snacks) in a little pile at his feet.
When I left, a guy was hitting the windshield with a baseball bat.

You go to the room, and the place you like to sit
is missing. This is an opportunity to trust, I suppose, or perhaps
for blind panic, if one were to consider this a metaphor
for something. But say it's not, say there are no such things
as metaphors for a moment, and where does that get you?
Presently, it gets me to a row of green and yellow plastic chairs,
those 1950s-looking ones I imagine Kenton would like
to collect. They're joined together by shiny metal clasps, chrome,
and the whole thing is full of sunlight through the plate-glass
window. It's the kind of scene I think of as lickable, how everything
looks like cheerful candy, and I wonder if there might be a way
to be there or here without a beginning, or without an ending,
or if perhaps there might be a concept for no middle.

IV

Now the scene changes, we say, and the next few years
are quiet. It's another curse, the inverse of the "interesting times"
the Chinese were said to go on so about. Nevertheless, there it is,
as the emptiness needs a something in order to be defined as empty,
which means we spend the next few years talking about other years,
as if that's what's important. Maybe that *is* what's important. It was terrible,
the hospital stay. The children. Not the children in the abstract way,
but those times worried that this would go wrong, or that, and then things
do go wrong and it almost feels like we'd wished for it to happen,
so not only do we have to go through this terrible time, but we also
have to keep reminding ourselves that we didn't wish for it. It's Problem
One. And there's our two-year-old son strapped to a board with an IV, crying.

And doesn't it feel like a formal device then? As if expecting it
were the same—or is the same—as willing it, but then almost willing it anyway,
saying something like, "Please God, or whoever, get it over with already . . ."
if the world isn't going to be a museum only, as museums keep calling out
that there's so much more to find in the past, like ourselves, for instance.
The simplification of our forms. The question of why it might be important
to save our dinnerware, or yo-yos. We have these accidents
in common: last night I was pulling a filing cabinet upstairs on a hand truck,
and at the ninety-degree turn it fell on top of me and I had to hold it like that,
one wheel on the stair, one in midair. So I had some time on my hands,
waiting for Robin to get home. They say that if you relax, lying there
is 80% as restful as sleep. And knowing how to relax is key, they say.

Here's a guess: we will sit on a wooden lawn chair in the sun, and we
will like it. We will run the numbers and think it sounds like a good
proposition. We will consult a map, even ask directions. The sun's
out right now, in fact, and it's all a matter of doing the next big thing.
Driving home, say. And then it's a manner of having done something.
Driving past the car wash. Yes, forcing a manner of doing the next
thing, which is filling out the accident report, while the old man
who hit my pickup is crying in the street. And then I'm walking around,
picking up the fender and light pieces and putting them in the bed.

V

Offers of help most often just end up complicating matters. That's been
a fundamental belief of mine for years, and has kept me
from asking for or offering help in many situations. On the other hand,
as long as one person is hungry, all people are hungry,
as Buckminster Fuller said, in a slightly different way. And then
I get to thinking maybe I should offer to help with that box
or whatever, but then I'd have to walk into your apartment,
wouldn't I, maybe tip over something in the dark
and end up married, or breaking something, or knowing something
I didn't want to know, as knowing things
brings a certain responsibility. Something always happens. We can't
get around it (which also always happens). So here I am.

But isn't it kind of insidious to offer to help someone? Isn't there
a scent of "what you're doing seems beyond you,
and I'm just the one to see you through this dark time"? Or
how about the spot I saw on TV a million years ago,
the staged scene, where a guy's breaking into a car, and people stop
to help. And the joke is that it's not his car. It was an experiment.
"People are always doing that," he says later
to the interviewer. Psychology 101. I just had some roasted and salted
pumpkin seeds that Jamie brought over. I liked them very much.
She was being nice. We buy things from Alex, her stepson,
that help him win trips through his school. They buy things
from our daughter Natalie, cookies mostly.

Making the world a better place also seems a worthwhile goal. But
better in what way? And in whose estimation? And what's the risk
that it would only lead to something worse? Which is the premise
behind many episodes of *Star Trek*, et cetera. The way "paper
or plastic" became such a tedious argument, that I decided
to eat only at restaurants, because I couldn't handle the pressure.
Well, not really, but I like saying that to friends. We're always
doing a variety of things, or vice versa, in a life full of doors one
through three. Doors are obsessed with us. One moment
you're standing there holding a box, and the next, what?

VI

What's the most earnest you've ever been? Perhaps this
is me at my most earnest. I have two children. At some point
I'll no longer be here, and I hope they still will. Mostly, though,
I'm not all that earnest otherwise. Earnest people tend
to make me feel vaguely antagonistic, as being earnest allows one
to say the ends justify the means, and mean it. They say things like
"nothing's ever enough," and I'm tired of nothing
ever being enough. But on both sides of whatever issue
there are these earnest people with these prepared noises
in a formal arrangement. It's a tennis match between two extremes
and the rest of us are the net. I watched a divorced couple once
fight over the top of a Toyota Starlet while passing off their son. Wednesdays
and every other weekend. The boy was crying. Everyone was crying.

I wonder if I cried when I was three and passed between my father
and mother in Portland, 1968. I've no memory of it,
and there's no one left to ask. We're really getting at
very little now, finally, back and forth, so that either of us could write
what the other one's going to say next in these arguments
and stories. And even that we tend to get used to, just as one gets
used to everyone being wrong about things. Or how
one gets used to that feeling when you just say something you're thinking
and the whole group rises to cheer for you. The first shock of it. The glow.

It's at a dinner party, and you flirt a little with your diet. Maybe you
make a joke about candles. This is conjecture. But dinner parties
leave one with formal constraints, even if there are infinite ways
those constraints can be expressed. The last one
I went to turned out to be a "group meeting" of some sort,
that I thought was to be a conversation about
what we think of America, but it was all really just a way
to try to get us to canvas for Democratic candidates
in our area. "Your friends and neighbors!" the young organizer said
with all the earnestness of revelation. It was one of the holidays,
the dinner party before that. We talked about death,

and I said so far, it's been easy not being a ghost. Margo
wouldn't even admit that much, saying that her family
was full of mostly dead people, who she's sure
write letters home explaining it all, but never send them.

VII

"Changes that are characteristic of a living room
include couches and wall treatments, but most commonly
begin with an eye toward the television, whether the orientation
of the seating would be toward optimal viewing
or interaction among people." There are a lot of things
we can make up like this that are probably true. It
makes me wonder why truth is so contested. It seems to come naturally:
the silver drawer opening and closing, and you might call it
music, and we can all kind of see the truth in that. And then we break
into a loveliness of water faucets and doors.

What you intend to do mixes quickly with ambient,
unintended things, and perhaps the car ride is better this way,
but the second thought comes that catches me up,
that "how many times can one move out from zero,"
which, from one perspective, isn't much of a question
at all. The answer is "yes," as it needs to be. But still, there are more times
than the present, much as it sounds nice not to think so, as the idea
of presents makes each day feel just like a birthday, right? The eternal
present that we keep hearing animals live in, or live
closer to . . . this place we're supposed to meditate toward,
as if counting cars as they pass goes one and then one and then one.

Once, at about 4:00 a.m., in my late twenties, while I was on my paper route,
I saw what looked like a giant mouse
hopping down the road, San Marcos, Texas. Then it looked like
a deformed deer, or some hybrid mouse-deer. So I pulled over
at the gas station and called the police. We're supposed to do that,
right? They asked me if it had pink spots
and if I'd been to a party. Turns out, it was a wallaby. Context
is everything. But then there's this other car ride, isn't there,
where I'm knowing it's the last moment with someone,
that it's the last moment we will still be in love, or something like it,
and the car door closing still sounds beautiful,
because it's a solid car. What was it Margo said once

about Jenny, back when we used to talk about Jenny?
"If one is admonished to do no one harm, is it implied
that it's OK to do no one any good either?"

VIII

Are we on the right track? Should it have been
the leaves in piles or the leaves in a row? And now, of course,
it turns out it's neither one, as Jamie from across the street
is currently mulching them for her garden
with her hose-mulcher, telling us it would have been even better
if they'd have been left where they fell, as that
would've allowed her to see the sticks and other things
more easily. Well, there you go. But then
it's anytime later, and we're asking ourselves if we're on the right track,
as we move around in a landscape of houses on the new bicycle path,
hoping that this is good exercise after reading that car exhaust
is slowly killing us. And what about that conversation
where we were going to find a lake, and ourselves suddenly
younger and on a weekend full of sex and watching the leaves turn?

Which is that all ways of disposing of leaves are metaphors
for death. An arrangement of leaves asserts a truth
as if the truth is firm and final; firmness and finality
are deathlike. Every raking that heads for a big pile and finds it, inevitably
finds mortality—and mortality is dreary. All the old
ways to pile leaves lead us to the same dark threshold. This includes
the ones that spell out "I love you" because the love
is shadowed by change and change is the livable version
of death. So Jamie's leaf-mulcher came along and invented
The Great Escape: leaves that evade endlessly. As long as she's out there
sucking them up, we're not dying! But there's always an opposite
kind of death—not the death of the pile of leaves
but the death of chasing them around. Or to put it in better terms,
not the death of completion but the death of sheer mess across the yard,
which is why people dissolve sooner or later, too. Jamie, out there,
is allowing me to say, "Oh well, let it go," whereas I keep looking
down the block at the little fires that seem to say, "Here is this good thing,
or this truth, and I refuse to let it go."

It's out there. We just need the right question that will make the right
answer suddenly appear, though this sounds like an overly airy way
of planning things. Most days we don't talk like this. We say things
like, "How many leaves do you think are out there, I mean
over the yard? How long do you think it would take us to count them?"

IX

"What would you like?" the waitress asks. And really,
is there no better question? It's another reason why I dislike
fast-food, especially fast-food drive thru lanes, where
they don't ask, "What would you like?" but rather "Would you like
to try a fabulous monster pack with wacky buns and
spider sauce for only $4.99 today?" so that I'm continually
having to start off my dining experience in a semi-adversarial
relationship. No. I want what I want, not what you want me
to want. So what would you like? What would please you the most?

One of *The Twilight Zone* episodes that keeps coming back to me
centers around a bad-guy getting gunned down in an alley
by the cops or something, but then waking up in a dive bar
where everything turned out perfect for him. Every pool shot
cleared the table. Everything perfect. He thought he was in
heaven. And then after a few more minutes of everything
going exactly his way perfectly, he wasn't able to get any interest up
for anything, and then realized, in the kicker,
that he was in Hell. "So what do you want?" It's half
of the elemental dichotomy: "What do you want?" "Who
are you?" And then a third, "Where are you going?" They
created the arc in the science fiction series *Babylon 5*.

My first father, the one who, I'm told, named me
Martin Lynn Enquist, Jr., from what I hear, played pool
for a living. Was it a job? If so, I'd think clearing the table
every time he hit the ball would be a pretty sweet proposition.
True, no one would play him then, but I bet they'd pay just
to see him clear the table every time. I know I'd pay to see that.
So what do I want? What does anyone want? My first dad, or my
second dad, the one who named me John Jerome Gallaher, Jr.,
what did they want? And did either get it? When I was adopted,
I called them New Mommy and New Daddy. Maybe I wanted that
and then got it. I really don't remember much about it,
which is pretty much what most of us say about most things.

X

The earth, friends, is doing fine. We're the ones in danger,
as X marks the spot upon which each of us is standing. And yes, we are
the center of the universe, but we've nothing much to show for it,
as everywhere else is also the center. Everything extends. Well,
there you go, then. So what else is inevitable? Like how many people
I don't know are going to call me, saying "John!" and then
try to sell me something, saying I'd then have something to show for it?
And that I might even impress my neighbors, be the envy
of the neighborhood. My brother, Richard, before he was adopted,
was named Richard Cory, and as he was nearly six, then, our new parents
left that as his name, no one saying anything about the suicide
of Richard Cory in either the Simon & Garfunkel or the Robinson
versions of "Richard Cory." As I was adopted at three, they changed
my name from Martin Lynn to John Jerome, no literary allusions there,
but I found out this year, late in my forties, that I probably wasn't born Martin
Lynn Enquist after all, that I was probably Eric Martin Enquist, or possibly
Lynn Martin Enquist. I think of the Chinese saying, that "The beginning
of wisdom is to call things by their right names," and wonder if that
has any bearing on my general distrust of most everything.

It's all practice, I guess, moving from a landscape to a souvenir, and then
from meditation to dream, and we catch a ride for a bit. See some trees.
We come back with a postcard and a T-shirt, and then the people
I've read about who have these premonitions that they won't come back,
and then don't. I don't want premonitions or coincidences. "Co-inky-dink,"
as we sometimes say, making it seem, for a moment, harmless. Fun,
even, to be lost or misplaced, or wanting to be.

DNA and the stars both make music, I've read, and sometimes
it can be quite affecting, a kind of furniture music of furniture itself.
But how does one decide when the composition is a composition?
And all these people who say they're attuned to it, OK, but those
who say they're keeping time, they certainly must know better, as there's
no keeping anything. And really, all those drills I used to go through in school
where I'd open my science book and put it over the back of my neck,

and curl into a ball under my desk, they were not really meant to help us
survive the disaster, but just to give us something to do, to
mimic being born maybe, and to practice saying, "I'm ready now."

XI

We do, as we say, what has to be done. The way things
are often, as we also say, at an impasse—when there's no way to go
but through another person
in much the same predicament. Does being a nice person
help? And have I been a nice person? We were driving around
this morning. I got some coffee from McDonald's.

Maybe it is what had to be done, as it's only logical
that some things must get done. But even with that,
there's always that little tick of a clock
that asks if the things we're doing
are strictly necessary. Looked at that way
it's hard to get a theory up about most things. The way
I had a theory of birds called *Retribution of the Landscape*,
after the third or fourth one pooped (shit?
did its business?) on me. It was the Fourth of July. I was
at a parade in a suburb of Minneapolis. It landed in my rainbow
snow cone. Last year, it landed on the back of my right hand
while I was riding my bicycle on a clear day in summer
in Indiana, Pennsylvania. And then again
just a few days ago on my left arm while at a dairy farm
on my daughter's second-grade field trip
where she tried flavored milk for the first time, saying,
"It's OK, but I like them better as steaks."

Should I be doing something differently? Then what
should it be? I'm at work again after being sick
yesterday. At least I felt sick in the morning,
and then I felt better. We take some things as signs
and others as simple events, the old occurrences-vs.-instances
conversation. In that way, I'm going to become
a different person soon (John XI maybe), as the probability of weather
or the probability of dinner. Or maybe I'm going
to remain this very same thing
continually. I'm not sure which fills me with hope,
and which terrifies me.

XII

Roman numerals don't do much for people
who like zero (oh, null, nil, or naught). Zero
was conceptual, as in Arabic numerals, where the whole thing
seems more conceptual, at least to me right now,
sitting here, trying to remember how to count
in Roman, let alone imagine subtraction, division,
et cetera. I was looking at the alphabet in my daughter's
second-grade classroom the other day,
wondering why the vowels were so
mathematically distributed: A bcd E fgh I jklmn
O pqrst U vwxyz. Vowel, three consonants, vowel, three
consonants, vowel, five consonants, vowel,
five consonants, vowel, five consonants (as long as you
ignore the uncertain status of Y, which reminds me
of the uncertain status of the zero [nulla, nihil]: how can
nothing be something? Indeed.).

"I have nothing to say and I am saying it," is perhaps
the most famous thing John Cage wrote, and he went on
to write seven or so books on the topic. I've always
enjoyed thinking of nothing as something, this
something called Nothing that one can hold. It turns
a lot of ghosts into people you can sit
and have dinner with. A guy I knew fifteen years ago,
named Todd Carman, felt like he
was becoming nothing. He'd tell me about it
while we rolled newspapers. He was the distribution
manager. He counted our papers. He always asked
inappropriate questions about women, as if
I'd know the answers. All I wanted was to get out
and throw my route. It was always 2:00 a.m.
back then. He was always inviting me over to his
place. He just seemed like another clueless
twenty-something, like we all were.

One night he didn't come in. He was busy
killing people, or trying to, with a .22-gauge
target rifle. It took thirteen shots to kill the one guy, I heard,
in his living room. The guy just stood there
trying to talk him out of it. He also killed the guy's
girlfriend, and he shot his own ex-girlfriend, Shannon,
a few times, once through the neck, but she
didn't die. She died two years later of an asthma
attack on the way back from Mexico, after having spent
several months in jail there for trying to buy diet pills.
What a life. Later, he said he heard them laughing downstairs,
and he knew, he just knew, they were laughing at him.

While they were bleeding out on the living room
rug, he shot several times into the wall, trying to get
to the apartment next door. Looking it up
just now, all I could find is:

     San Marcos Daily Record.
     Carman, Todd. Shooting spree, 7/12/91

When he ran out of energy, he called his brother
and then went out on the front step, where his brother
met him, and waited with him for the police.

XIII

How many people haven't you married, that you thought
for a moment—who knows—maybe you would? It seems to me
right now that one should take such things
as warnings, but of exactly what, I'm not sure. We should all
be allowed to feel this near miss, how many things happen
at the same time, and how people have varying degrees
of perceiving that. That could be the warning. Or just
that "you never know." Or better, that line by Chuck Berry:
"It goes to show you never can tell." And so and so,
and so and so. But even with all the parsing, at some point
there will only be one person left. When my uncle died, for instance,
he was playing cards with my aunt. It was his move
and she just thought he was thinking. If so,
he's been thinking a long time. When she died a few years later,
I don't know who was there. Someone she loved,
I hope. And if not that, at least someone.

I hit a possum once, late at night on my paper route,
1990. I stopped and looked back at it lying there
in the road—a patch of blood on its head. Then slowly
from the bushes past the curb, several more
possums appeared. They went to the one I hit. It
almost looked like a ceremony, light as a feather,
stiff as a board, or something. And the possum rose to its feet,
wobbling a bit, and followed them back into the bushes.

At some point that one thing will be for certain:
we're standing in line. I picture us there
as if at an airport waiting for our various flights
to be called. And from my spot in line, I worry
about the people around me, like when Natalie
was at her first sleep-over. Mostly I worry
that she'll be comfortable, and that she won't
feel lost. Eliot, who's three, was lost for a while
the other night. I was in the kitchen

reading John Cage's *SILENCE*, and he
was playing in the living room as the house
grew a little dark, and then I heard him call out,
"Hey guys. Hey, where did everybody go?"

XIV

I just forgot how to count in Roman numerals, and had to look it up.
I used to be good at them, and would always wait for the end of TV shows,
where I'd get to count the date. The game was: figure out the date
before it blinked away. In that, it was like most other things. It was
an odd feeling, when it went from MCM to MM. I'd been seeing MCM
my whole life. Natalie was born in MMI, November the 16th,
after the Twin Towers were already gone, and most likely
all she'll know is MM. M & M. *Mmm mmm good.*

We all know in the abstract to be prepared for several eventualities,
most of which won't happen. And so what do we do with all these preparations
we never have to use? All the driving routes one imagines
in case one has to get to these people or to those people. What to say
when all these people call who never call. And in the same way,
there's always something that we can't imagine preparing for, that happens.
Quick! Say something memorable! At every point it's a matter of minutes
and then seconds, then now, the stopwatch winding down the hundred-year flood
that becomes the flood you're steeping in. Still, thinking about it, it begins
to look like: one, two, three, many . . . many, three, two, one. And that's
a terrible way to count, when most days it's routine maintenance,
and every cup of coffee a suite for spoon and porcelain. *Being*
is the true subject, right? And they say there's a hole in every theory of being.

"Do you think you'll ever be free?" was just asked on CNN, by Soledad O'Brien,
I think. And there we are. Everywhere is locked in with everyone, as
almost no one makes it out, as Jason Molina says. But let's pretend
for a moment that we have choices, that these eventualities are a choice,
as if the Camptown ladies might be able to do anything other than sing their song.
And then, would anything change? It's the old question, because the universe,
to a being of infinity, is wholly known, which includes the sci-fi stuff,
where an astronaut gets going a little too fast in *2001: A Space Odyssey*,
and ends up a little ahead of the speed of light, suddenly finding himself
everywhere at once, including a quiet white room, like this one I'm in right now,
contemplating breakfast. While doing that, why not check in on the ladies
in Camptown? Connect all the dots of the connect-the-dots at once?

But once you're infinite, as infinity is travel, what happens if you slow down again? Or is it that once crossed, it's a line from which there's no return?

XV

It's a nice idea, to think we might have no effect
on what happens, as that allows a theater to erupt
around us. When I was in my late twenties, my cousin Lyle died
like he was in a movie. He was ferrying a small plane—
a Piper, I think—from somewhere north
down to Houston. While flying over Kansas, he radioed the lead plane
to say, "Hey, let me show you what this thing can do," and he proceeded
to attempt a loop-the-loop,
which clipped the lead plane and tore the rear ailerons from his plane,
effectively turning the Piper into a rock. My parents
didn't tell me about it until a few months after his funeral. They were worried
I'd be upset. They bought me some mint chocolate chip
ice cream at Baskin Robbins. And it was rather like a theater,
one where we can sit there in the fluorescent lighting
with our ice cream, wondering if at some point
we might ever become immune to our parents,
while it melts down our fingers.

I was adopted close to my fourth birthday, in October,
I think. Just before Halloween, when I dressed up
as Casper. I flew in on Continental Airlines ("with the golden tail"),
from Portland to Wichita (Kansas, again, which is probably
why I'm thinking about it) and a new name. Who was Martin
shall now be John. And I can imagine one of these names
as my stage name, and the other my mild-mannered alter ego.

I've read that thinking such things is common
for people who were adopted. Or maybe just
for people in general, as we all exist on an arc
of behavior. The disconnectedness of being adopted,
that there's always this hole, this unresolved bit. I
don't know. I feel rather disconnected from such theories.
Better, I think, is this idea I read once years ago
that for every event that goes one way, the universe splits
so that it can go the other way as well. I wonder then

whatever happened to Martin and to Lyle. They were very young in their different ways. They hardly knew anything.

XVI

The early bird might get the worm, but the early person
mostly just has to sit around and wait for everyone else to show up.
So much for pithy ideas about personal betterment. People
have always been like this, I'm certain, waking up one day
feeling a little different (6% Neanderthal, maybe), and then wondering
if this means it's the end of something or the beginning of something.
I'm better now, this morning, not realizing I'd been worse,
a light cold. So maybe this is the worse to some future better? The idea
of becoming enters, and so then we're all becoming.

In the movie *The In-Laws*, there's this scene where the fathers of the bride
and groom are running through gunfire at an airport, and the
secret-agent dad calls out to the common-man dad, "Serpentine!
Serpentine!" while zigzagging. For some reason that's stuck with me more
than most anything else from my youth. It felt like good advice,
as the unknown is merciless, and so of course, the common-man dad
runs back to his starting place and begins again, running through the bullets
a second time, getting it right. Repetition is how we learn things,
as Natalie and Eliot both are asking me for the same story over and over,
until it starts to feel to me as if there's no other story than this one.

When did I become what I've become, then, as it always seems
nothing's changing? "Life is what happens to you while you're busy
making other plans," as John Lennon had it, and I stood
in front of the Dakota in the cold, on the anniversary of his murder.
I thought I was paying attention. Maybe I should have paid something else
then. Some more subtle division, as three years after writing this
I'm looking back at it: it's 2012 now, we've moved across town, after
our neighbor, Matt, tried to corner Robin in our basement while I
was out of town. There's a question in that, and the answer comes
when you stop asking the question. We sit around, and windows
are what we talk about, because we're surrounded by windows. Life's
a game of Hide & Seek, they say, and maybe you'll be a really good hider.

XVII

In another sense, we're foreign to each other. We say we're
communicating, or that we hope to be communicating, and all
I can think of is that I could've chosen that other chair over there.
I even thought about it, as I'm often ambivalent about where to sit.
I find, though, that I seem to end up in just about the same place in rooms
as always. Is it just out of politeness? Routine? Something
about our characters, maybe: Where You Sit Is Who You Are.
And what if some of these people are harboring some secret grudge
or desire to be in a different seat? They could mention it,
but they'd just look petty. We could offer, but we'd look
condescending. No, really, take my seat. I want you to have it.

Seems to me right now that's the level of most questions, and most
conversations. We're all people sitting together at 2:00 a.m.
in some bright kitchen, this close to everything falling apart. It
reminds me of all those charts and graphs about the safest seat
on a plane I've seen. Precisely where the plane is going to break
apart; who becomes wreckage, and who ends up like the guy in a flight crash
movie I saw years ago played by Ron Glass (who also played Ron
Harris on *Barney Miller*), still wearing his gray business suit, who walks away
from the crash site unharmed, but confused, not able to figure out
why his watch has stopped. How many ways are there of going
through this door, and then, which door. . . . "Can I get a witness?"
right? Isn't that what we're supposed to say next?

In another sense, we're just as foreign to ourselves. We're each
a universe of microbes, which just made my son laugh
and my daughter go take a shower, which she was going to do anyway.
We were looking at a magazine, *Science Illustrated*, at a full-page picture
of a biofilm. And we have to trick ourselves, as well, so I set all the clocks
in the house fifteen minutes ahead, as I bet a lot of people do. Someone
I used to know well would set the alarm in a different room, so that
[he or she] would have to get up when it went off. But Jenny, I'll
name her, would just as often then fall asleep on the couch. I
love that story, or perhaps I just loved her, even if I made her up.

XVIII

"All animals have interests," I'm reading in an overview
of philosophy. And so there we are, scanning the horizon. Ideas,
as well as beliefs, can become a compass—which can be as helpful
as it can be damaging, without knowing which it's going to be
beforehand, and then also so difficult to know after, as well.
It might be better to stay away from both, and wander, or
would we be just like birds then, flying into plate-glass windows?

"Birds!" Amanda says, in that tone that says
she's still sick of hearing everyone talking about birds all the time,
as if suddenly we could get over our need to project ourselves
outward to things that float or hover or are otherwise
beyond our understanding. It happens in the distance,
what holds our interest, I've heard, scanning the horizon. At least
that's what they say of Americans, the large future of our desire.
I saw a diagram once of how cultures see themselves. Some
the large past. Some the large now. And some, like America, the large
tomorrow. I wonder, as that was twenty years ago,
if it's still that way. Or if we're losing that future. If maybe we're
turning, or have already turned, to the past, where my brother
visited me once after college, during his military years,
and I drove him through Houston, playing the radio loud. I turned
the wrong way down a busy one-way city street, and we were suddenly
in one of those movies. He was the straight man climbing up
on his seat while I got to be the foil, the cartoon brother,
both of us going, "AAAAAAAAAAA."

When Amanda leaves the office next spring, she'll be the last
of the students to leave that I've known all my time here.
So I'm hanging Post-it notes around the office for something to do:
*What do you love about the world and why? What do you hate about the world
and why?* "It has to be a real thing, not an abstraction," I tell her,
because these days I'm feeling like real things. She hates birds, currently,
but maybe that's just her reflection in the mirror as she's going
from wall to wall, taking down these Post-it notes. She's
getting married in a year. He'll die in four.

XIX

It's our Indian Summer weekend, coming up.
It might even get as high as eighty degrees. It was a cold October,
I thought, and fairly wet, too. Such things are always better
with friends around, we say, as I feel like I'm not as close to people
as I once was. Maybe that's just perspective,
or distance. A friend of Roger's son died a couple weeks ago,
and it was ruled, in the end, an accidental overdose,
not suicide. I always thought my cousin Lyle
would go that way. Maybe that's the most shocking thing
about finding out he crashed a plane into Kansas, nearly
fifteen years ago now. Today I got word, as coincidences go,
that there's going to be a bell-ringing for Britnee Baldridge
this Saturday, a student I had last year who died
last month. She suffocated in her bed after an epileptic seizure.
I went to the folders from the class last week,
to maybe see something she wrote, but for some reason her folder
wasn't there. It was the only one missing.
She sat in the front row, a little to my right.

Once, sometime around 1990, on my paper route,
when I was driving through town at 3:00 a.m., rolling the papers as I went,
I passed the funeral home. All the lights were off,
but the front door was open. What's the secret message? There's
supposed to be one, like in those "connect all the dots with only three
straight lines" problems we were given in school to find out
if we were geniuses. The trick is what to ignore.

Robin told me at lunch that someone put a water pitcher
in her mailbox. She has no idea why. So what is she
going to do with it? It's cheap, and already an abstraction,
like how my first father is an abstraction, who made it to just about
twenty-five, and a couple months ago
I was contacted by a guy who's twenty-five
who turns out to be my son. One for one. And I've no idea
what they said about Lyle at his funeral, so
good-bye, Lyle, you know?

XX

The prompt is that you're supposed to imagine
your favorite food, and then make it a person, starting
at its death, and then pass it to the person on your left,
so I choose you. Such things are practice questions, I guess, if
I want to figure out why we're doing this, in the way pets
are practice children, or practice mourning our deaths.
Maybe the question, then, is between, "Is the world
something you need to get past?" or "Is the world something
you need to accommodate yourself with?" Or maybe
the question is to find out if there's a difference between the two.

Richard just stopped by. He's off to lunch, where he's going
to have his last "solid" before the procedure tomorrow,
so he's going to miss the office thing tonight. We talked a little
about doing research. He likes it. I'm ambivalent. I wish I had more
to say at times like this, something concrete, as I know he's talking
about research because he doesn't want to think about
what "the procedure" might mean. To say or to share, even "Hell, yes!"
or "Damn fine!" All I could think of is I just noticed a while ago,
walking with Robin, that the little red wax string that used
to help one open a Life Savers pack seems to no longer
be there. When did that happen?

I just thought to say that I was dragged into a large vacant lot once,
Orange County, California. It would've been first grade,
the year the toddler next door drowned in their swimming pool,
coffin the size of a suitcase. I don't remember
anything more about whatever happened, other than I was dragged
into a plywood fort by some other kids, a plywood lid, basically,
to a hole in the ground. To make it a metaphor, I've often felt since
that I'm being dragged someplace, and I'm never sure
if it's against my will or not. And how we keep saying things,
like, "I left them where I thought they'd be safe." We
went to Disneyland thirty-five times while living there,
and one time I got stuck for forty-five minutes on the Pirates of the Caribbean

ride, right at the "Yo ho, yo ho, a pirate's life for me" bit. There are many levels to negative experiences, and you remember the ones you think about. No one's sure where the rest go.

XXI

In heaven, according to Kurt Vonnegut's
play *Happy Birthday, Wanda June*, you are
whatever age you were your happiest. Maybe it
wasn't in that play, now that I'm thinking
about it. Well, it was in one of his (or Kilgore Trout's) plays
or books. And I wondered what age I would be there. We all
give ourselves a story to base the narrative of our lives
upon. Let's say we tried to draw circles when we were ten
and our circles were terrible. And then it's one long series
of wobbly completeness. Where to go next?
Let's hope it's a romantic comedy.

Brenda was saying last night that she still has a long list of things
she wants to do and she now realizes, as she's close to fifty,
she'll not do them all. Is it more a problem of the past,
or a problem of the future, how perhaps one makes
impractical lists of what one wants to do with one's life
or one travels along without proper attention
to what one is meaning to be doing. "Meaning," and
"to be doing" have always been problems for me. Let's say
for a minute you're fifty. Where are you going to live
and what are you going to look like? Let's say now
that you're ten. Same thing. You never know.
And then here we are at a blackboard, everyone watching
and we're attempting our first big circle.

And then there's the flip side, all those other things one does
that don't seem to matter much in Vonnegut's heaven. Both
of my brothers-in-law have spent time in jail, and now
Ben, the oldest, a year or so younger than I am, is in a clinic
of some sort after blowing out the bank account on drugs,
leaving his wife and young daughter destitute, the house in foreclosure,
a little pile of bad checks. Addiction is stronger than love,
some say. Who knows? I'm thinking about his daughter. Her name
is Celeste, meaning "heavenly," from the Latin, and the name of

Babar the elephant's wife. "There's no place to go but up,"
hopeful people say at times like this, but really
there are many directions things can go at any time.

XXII

"When Yer Twenty-Two" is an early song from The Flaming Lips,
and also the kicker in a poem from A. E. Housman, number XIII
in *A Shropshire Lad*. I don't remember much about being twenty-two,
in much the same way that I don't remember much
about being most ages, and how I find myself constantly
in these little arguments with Robin or whomever about what age
anyone was at any given time doing most anything,
and what we did or didn't do or which one of us it was.

What we all have in common about being whatever age we are
though, is that we can be certain we'll spend most of our time waiting.
And for me, I can also be fairly certain I'll have a headache later,
like right now for instance, though no one can ever figure out why . . .
that light glaze that sweeps the inside of the skull, back to front, the long
preamble to an elusive point, as we continue to sit here trying not
to shuffle in our chairs, waiting for eternity, contemplating
the irony of every sentence containing the word "eternity" or
"everything" or "forever" or "timeless" or "nothing." Still, though,
they're stubborn, these sentences, and enjoy visiting us in the night.

Once, five or so years ago, when I was thirty-whatever
my left pupil popped into full dilation one morning,
and stayed that way. It didn't hurt or anything, it just stayed
real big no matter what the lighting conditions. So I went to
an eye doctor, and he tried for a while to fit me with glasses
until it dawned on him that my pupils weren't behaving
in unison. He then asked if there was a history of brain tumors
in my family. Turned out later to be nothing, a virus, as most things
do, until something turns out to be something, as an inevitable
surprise. But either way, this time, I got to wait a couple weeks
thinking my number was up, but it wasn't. Just one more
station along the route. Just another happy customer.

XXIII

One of the best things about life
is that you don't have to understand it
to catalog it. It's another part
of our conversation about usefulness. It's a
beautiful day, today, for instance. Seventy-two degrees
suddenly after a week of winter. There's no use
understanding that, nothing to understand
really. It's just weather.

I've seen a lot of it. When I was young we moved
constantly. I like to add that it was one step
ahead of the law, but it wasn't. It was just my father
changing jobs. Going to a new city. So in rapid succession
it was Portland, Wichita, Orange County
California, Birmingham, and then Long
Island. I've always tried to sidestep questions like
"Where are you from?" as I always feel like they'll
think I'm trying to be difficult by saying, "Well,
a lot of places," as if I'm trying to
be mysterious or something. Or as if
I'm trying to make some comment about not being
defined. Maybe places do define us. Maybe we get used
to the weather there, as everywhere I've ever lived they've
had some phrase about how the weather
is especially changeable in that place. "Just wait
around fifteen minutes and it'll change." That sort of thing.

That's another of the ways things don't seem to change
much, the more they change, like the cousin we all
seem to have who brings a different wife to each
family reunion. So is there ever growth? Healthier ways
of coping with the sorts of things life does
over and over? How they never mention waiting around
that extra minute, that sixteenth, to where
it's all back at square one, and just what you expected.

XXIV

"Is being aware of our limitlessness freeing or restraining?" I just
read. That's one way to start off the day. Amanda, for
instance, just said, "Limitlessness? Who has that?" And I
said something about the "limitless potential
of the human mind," to which she replied, "Birds?"

"And though they were sad, they rescued everyone,"
as Wayne Coyne had it on *The Soft Bulletin*, whose original
title was *The Soft Bullet In*. Two more versions of
getting the message. We're sad, and here we go. I needed
rescuing a bit when I was eleven and wandering in the woods
when we lived in Birmingham, right around the Bicentennial.
I always felt then that the Bicentennial was going
to be something people would talk about forever. I
swear now, I don't think I've heard anyone mention it once
since then. But then, at least, the little line of woods
that followed a little river felt pretty limitless to me,
especially when we were wading in the river up near our waists
and we came across a real live car half in, half out of the water.

It's supposed to get all Hollywood after that, right? And someone's
supposed to get eaten by the trunk full of snakes or something,
but nothing much happened. We ate some sandwiches. Later,
we climbed a steep rise of shale that kept coming apart beneath us,
fifty or so foot drop. It was all good fun up until my brother
nearly took my finger off by hitting it with a brick that he was
trying to throw down a manhole, and I ran home with a palm
full of blood and finger. It's a scar now, along the inside of the joint
of my right index finger. It's one in a series, isn't it? Bulletin
after bulletin. And some of these scars go away over time. I
wasn't expecting that, that some fade, so that we're all going along
some path, whistling as best we're able, and then
some leave to the left and some to the right, like birds, right?
On a telephone wire? And then you and then me.

XXV

To review, I'm thinking that cataloging one's life is a sort of other-living,
a creepiness, like those people who go everywhere videotaping
themselves or their kids or cute ducks in a field of flowers
which becomes a substitute for doing something, so that the video later
is the event and not event-residue that we skim onto our shelves
for some imagined later. Put it all together and you have a picnic,
I just thought, but exactly why I thought of that I'm not sure.
Something to videotape, I guess, like a replacement for the sex tape
everyone always thinks they're going to make but most never do,
thankfully, as it would all just become "Earthrise As Seen
from All the Junk We Left on the Moon."

Long past the life or not-life, this is your life—a repeat
of a sixty-year-old TV show that's now fifty light years on its way
past Alpha Centauri . . . how we've been able to say such things
with greater and greater distances factored in
for a while now (sixty-year-old TV show!), and the people
from those shows all mostly dead now. But that's only the video parts,
the rest of the days are still there too, they tell us, in sliceable diagrams
of how time is thought to maybe work, like a loaf of bread,
with all those days that don't lead anywhere but the next day,
half-distracted by everyone else's reflections in the picture window
behind a little row of yellow and green scoop chairs, as they move
in all directions and begin to feel like communal autobiography.

Today's chapter is starring The Interpretive Welcome Center
that rises before me as I'm driving into Nebraska. A little
interpretation is nice, thank you. I like that, promising something more
than just an accurate accounting, proper citation, with a free map
and the sound environment of a Walmart,
where it always feels like it's late night, "My Life" playing
over the sound system, as I'm wondering
absentmindedly whatever happened to Billy Joel. He wants us
to go ahead with our own lives. He wants us to leave him alone.

XXVI

What does it mean to be useful? To be a useful person? My son's
watching Thomas the Tank Engine, where the goal is ever
to be useful. So how would I fare? When one balances accounts,
how do any of us fare? I have this ongoing joke with Robin
that she's the kind of driver who would drive off the road if a car
was heading her way, just to give them more room. Good news
for the road. And wear your seat belts and stay within ten of the speed limit.

So what anecdote will pull me through this time? There must be one
that starts off something like, "This one time I helped _____
do _____." All that comes to mind right now though
is that I've helped some people move, I guess. I loaned Roger my truck
now and then. Kenton, too, a couple times. But that's not much
for effort. Roger even walked all the way over to get it. Well, we
have Rebecca's and Tim's furniture in the garage, waiting for a garage sale
we keep saying we were going to have, but it's been there two years
now. I feel suddenly like baking cookies for someone. Or spaghetti
or something, as Jamie's back picking up more of our leaves. I know
she's getting something out of it, as she's going to use them in her garden,
but she's also doing us a favor. Once, I helped Brendan with his car.
1984. He needed license plates to get it home one night (it was uninsured
and unregistered), so I took one off the front of a neighbor's car,
telling him he should bring it back sometime, imagining it kind of like
borrowing, but I found out from him twenty years later that he never did,
until he got pulled over months later. Turns out, there was a warrant
out for me in New York after that, at least Brendan thinks so,
and a judge ordered him to stay away from me, as part of his sentence.

I've always really liked that "Be on my side / I'll be on your side" bit
from Neil Young's "Down by the River." Sounds good to me, if one
can skip the murder that comes in the second verse, and just make it be
that we're running for no reason, or maybe running to help, something
fantastic: news to the orphanage maybe, or delivering a package that went
to our place by mistake. We've plenty of stuff to grill. And cold drinks.
If you're ever in Maryville, look us up. We have a punch line, or maybe
a line from a children's learning song, for an address: 1 2 3 4 Chick.

XXVII

"There are flowers in the dirt
and there's dirt in your eyes," as the saying goes
that I just made up. Is this what thinking is like? I've been thinking
for forty-four years or so, and I'm not sure, as most thinking doesn't resolve—
and most thinking is laid over the top of other thinking—
and thinking is fairly continuous—all process—in our
"getting somewhere" costumes, as Rae Armantrout says. In that way
most thinking is like most lives, accruing by accident,
irresolvable. It's why we're said to come back as ghosts, right?

I've always had a hard time with people just sitting
there not saying anything. If people aren't talking
then I have to guess what they're thinking
and I always guess something like, "this guy
talking to me sure is an idiot." So, over the years,
I've tended to stay far away from such people. I imagine them all
in a room somewhere, quietly, with their private thoughts. And then
comes the inevitable question about where
this thinking is leading us, where we're getting to, and all these ideas
of going somewhere, as if there were anywhere
to get to, with a little bouquet of flowers on it, when mostly
our thinking out loud is just us being friendly.

The other day Natalie (I'm putting this in a year later. She's
nine now) said to Robin, "Did you see that? There was just a man
standing by the couch in a suit." And no, Robin
hadn't seen anything. A few days before, I was walking down the front hall
and somehow the papers I was carrying shifted in my hand
as if someone were behind me, giving them a little tug. Robin says
the kitchen cabinets sometimes open and close in the night,
and the other day a plate fell off the shelf into the kitchen sink. So,
with that, Halloween is over. We're coming up on the
holiday season. For Natalie and Eliot, as they're children,
that's a place to get to. Still, I'm not dreading it. The sun's
coming out. It'll get to seventy today. How you can look

at the weather sometimes and it can appear to be washing away
who we were. How in high school I played clarinet. Second chair.

XXVIII

"It changes you," they say about a lot of different things,
but what they don't say is that most people
change right back. And then it's time
to make a different point. To quiet that
into this other thing. There are many ways
to quiet the mind, most of them involve noise,
which I find charming. Music,
for instance, which is a space within which
we participate with our bodies. And then
the TV. Or music and the TV. Or the static of memory.

And then we talk about it. It's more fun
just to talk about the idea of us
talking, sometimes. Like the other night,
Brenda said, "Who's John Cage?" I thought
everyone knew who John Cage was. I keep having
the idea that whatever my experience has been,
it's been the same for everyone, and I keep
being shown otherwise. It reminds me
of a thought I had the other day: how clear
can you be, when the point you're trying to make
is that clarity is impossible? Like when I was a Boy Scout
in Birmingham, Alabama, 1976 or so. We
were on a campout where the scoutmaster
was working on a hollowed-out bedpost he'd filled
with lead. He was burning *NIGGER KNOCKER*
and *GET RUNNIN* up the opposing sides. It changes you,
they say. Sure, but how is never certain. And what was I
supposed to do with that one? I was eleven.

And how sometimes when people are talking,
it all seems to me so much a part of a ritual,
I can get the picture that one of us is sitting
on the other's lap, and one of us
is causing the other to speak,

but carefully, invisibly, so that either one of us
might be either, or that only one of us
is there at a time. There are people around,
looking uncomfortable. "Are we the audience,"
they ask, "or witnesses?"

XXIX

"The idea just came to me one day," or, better,
"It just dawned on me." Either way, we're all admonished
to beware our tendencies, as apparently tendencies
tend to wind us down or blind us to better things our tendencies keep us
from noticing—I imagine that becoming a tendency
so that potentially all tendencies aren't bad
just as all goals aren't good. We could go round
saying, "it continued to dawn on me," or
"I have a tendency to dawn on me."

I remember something like that from high school,
where we were in our goal-setting class, and the teacher kept telling us
not to let our lives go by without setting goals, and I asked him,
what if the goals aren't good ones, like to hurt people
or to do bad things, might it not have been better
not to have goals? I don't remember what happened
after that. Nothing much, I'm certain, but he did talk about
brushing teeth next, how he was always told to brush up and down,
and he did that religiously for years, and now (this was
1982 or 1983) his gums were receding—so we shouldn't
brush that way, we should brush
in circles. Maybe that could be a goal even.

"Why not be straightforward," we always say
back and forth, but once we get past "pass the salt,"
things get confused with where are we going
and what are we doing. What are the relevant
and irrelevant bits, when most people
make up mostly what they think people
are trying to say to them, and they're usually right enough
for communication to be said to have taken place,
though where it takes the place is everybody's guess. Even so,
the important thing to remember is that an effective brushing
cleans every exposed tooth surface in a gentle, massaging motion,
and most people think they brush for at least a minute

or two, but in reality they brush for thirty seconds
or less. Time yourself and see how you
do. An effective brushing, they say, takes two to three
minutes. And flossing, as well, helps protect your gums.

XXX

I've just been invited to read "A Book of Truths
Revealing God's Plan for Humanity. It will Change the Way you
View your Life and the World around you. It's the Beginning
of the Awakening," which I'm going to add
to my list of things that might make us different
from other animals. They're always saying
what it is that makes people different from
non-people—the latest one I saw recently
was dancing. Apparently humans have rhythm
and other creatures don't (except for some birds, which
might explain part of our fascination). But I've also noted
many other things that make us different,
movies, for one. And I've never seen an animal
give another advice. Well, maybe I have, come to think of it,
in rather elemental ways. The "eat or be
eaten," lesson that is the cornerstone of any good
management philosophy. Do animals tell jokes?

Traffic continues. How long does a day seem
to a cat? I wonder if it's similar to how I feel when I'm
invited to "please wait here while you wait." It is certainly possible
that I cross the room and think, "If what you're doing
causes sounds, are you making music?" The way
elephants are always painting or joining
bands. What we're trying to do is always interrupted
by what someone else is trying to do. Lisa threw a glass
of red wine on me once at a party in Athens, Ohio,
and I never got to figure out why. I didn't even know her
well. And then love was Brendan MacNaughton throwing rocks
up to Jackie Bakker's window in high school,
middle of the night, just like in the movies, only she was
thinking it a different kind of movie and called 911,
so we had to scatter, and I hid in the bushes
while the police questioned him.

"I still wish I knew why she did that," is a phrase
a lot of people could say about a lot of other people. It's the
same feeling I get when I'm reading a book that holds my
attention, and then I finish it, and just kind of sit there
looking around with suddenly nothing to do.

XXXI

Whenever I see the Roman numeral XXX
I think of pornography. Probably many people do? And what
do the number of Xs really matter in rating movies
anyway? I imagine a panel of judges behind a fold-up table,
like something from a wedding reception, bored
(which is any sameness on its way to being maddening),
watching all these people doing all the things imaginable . . .
and then they, what? Deliberate? Well, this one really should be
an X, but not an XXX, because, well, and then comes
some dry description of whatever—or are there
such distinctions? Is XXX a real designation anyway? I suppose
I'd look it up, but do I really want to know? People might think
I'm a film buff or something, and I've really never been much
interested in film. Or TV, really.

When did I lose interest in that? How did it occur? Was it
a process? Like getting over loss? Seven stages, maybe? And then
now here I am in this one? Number seven maybe? Or really,
should there even be seven stages, or is that just the TV
version? Maybe that's more like it. I think I dislike them
because of how easily I find myself manipulated by them,
just as they're mostly so clumsy about it, especially if there's a lot of blood
and people in pain. Why would I want to pay money
for that? I saw my uncle Herm die. It was the groan of air
and the whole thing with the body letting go. After the ambulance took him
there was this problem of where each of us should stand. I ended up
in the backyard with my cousin Lyle, looking at the retaining wall
made from concrete and glass bottles.

Terri's husband Mark is in constant pain. And I don't know
how Brenda is doing. I think she's still on chemotherapy.
I haven't heard, and it would seem like prying to ask. Comedies
are different. When people laugh they look younger.
Sometimes things happen, as things are always happening,
and it becomes imperative to laugh and to look younger.

XXXII

The other night we drove downtown and something was on fire
somewhere. We could smell it and see smoke, but
we couldn't tell exactly where it was. A little to the east and south
of the parking lot, I think? We even saw a couple flakes of ash
floating around the car as we parked. No one else seemed to notice
or to be bothered by it, so we decided to go on in to the restaurant.
And how curious should we be is the question, or one of the
questions. Maybe Question Three. And "Nothing to see here folks,"
is the official reply. The burning bush is speaking to someone
else, about other things. We say it doesn't matter, but we know
there are always things that matter, just around the corner.

Earlier, I saw outside our building they were picking up leaves
with a pull-trailer the size of a Volkswagen, but with
a bigger top. It had TORO written on the side, and it was hitched
to a mini-tractor. It was impressive and loud, as people with leaf blowers
foraged around it, blowing leaves into its path. It's burning
season. We're allowed to burn things twice a year now,
in town. There are two days left, so today I'm going to
finish the burn pile I started burning yesterday. When we
first bought the house, there were two brush piles, each
easily the size of that TORO. It took me two months, on weekends,
to get them burned down. In them, I found a dead rabbit, a deer leg,
and several children's toys. One, a Hot Wheels yellow pickup truck,
I still have. I gave it to Eliot. Back then it didn't matter
when we burned, or what, I guess. Now we've *rules*.

It seems there's always someone who has just returned
from years away to wherever I am, and that person is always ready
to check off all the changes that they find. The Holiday Inn
is new. They took down the water tower. I've done that
a few times myself, I guess. But even so, I find it both
interesting, in a Historical Society kind of way, and also
kind of uncomfortable, like having dinner with one's spouse's
first husband or wife, et cetera, watching his or her mouth,

watching it move, watching it chew. And playing games with the forks. Folding and refolding the napkins.

XXXIII

All faces tend to have a permanent expression,
and it grows more pronounced as one gets older,
until it's nearly all one can manage most days. I wonder
what mine is. Thinking such things, I've heard, is the beginning
of what often causes us to change in some fundamental way
that's invisible to anyone else but ourselves. Should
we then despair? Would anyone notice if we did?

This is section XXXIII, the Jesus age. And Natalie, one week
from her eighth birthday, says I'm full of bad ideas,
but I look around and can see plenty of other people with bad ideas
as well. It's good not to be alone. We seem to,
as a species, cultivate bad ideas with great fecundity. Our
bad ideas, like our children and our pets, that never seem all that bad
to us, but which are usually instantly recognizable
to everyone around, mirror reality then, as there are always many new things
to do, and there are always fewer ideas than we think there are.

Let us consider the humble banana. It seems to be
at a critical point in its history, as it faces a crisis
of diversity, which is, there isn't any. I read recently
that something's going to happen and suddenly
they're all going to be gone. That would be depressing. And
what would we give then to the monkeys? That's
probably the least of the consequences, but not to
monkeys, who also use tools and have all sorts of drama
going on in their social circles, many of which
are probably bad ideas . . . But all things must, as the Bible
and George Harrison agree, pass away. And wasting time, I've heard,
as in the time it takes to have a bad idea, turn it over, and
move on, turns out to be useful too, in a finger exercises
sort of way, so now I am perhaps being useful, and, as we all know,
it's good to be useful. And it's not so much that we go
at some point, but that we're swept away by our desire,
or perhaps by a giant broom. Imagining that, just now,

made Natalie laugh, and we ran around the living room going "whoop-whoop," for some reason, flapping like chickens.

XXXIV

If things contain their opposites, why bother? That suffices, I guess,
to get a certain type of party going, or to get another type of party
to come to a screeching halt. More like a pregnant pause, most likely,
suggesting a medical term for it. And what other important questions
are there, after that? What to name the baby? Who's the father?

Moving along and being nice to other people helps. For instance,
say we're at the hospital. Depending on how one thinks
of such things, we could be most anywhere. Say we're in Maryville,
Missouri, then, and we bring all of history along, some way
to care for each other. And the other history, the one
that no one knows about, we bring that too. Now we're all there,
and there's my MRI to look at. And music above us
somewhere, so that every now and then
we get the feeling it's a production number, where we can hide
awhile from literature, and the peppy music bodes well for us
as we catch ourselves humming along about going through the desert
on a horse with no name. Or, a few years earlier,
we're in the emergency room for the first time with our first child,
who's sick, and her temperature spikes to 104. We're terrified
in the same way everyone else is terrified.

The point is always this. The pianos are all prepared differently,
but served the same way. Something must remain
constant. And it's nice to think of us there humming along,
with perhaps a bit of lyric, as if the whole point of our lives
was to travel a great distance to fill these four minutes and eleven seconds
with this peppy song where it feels good to be out of the rain.

XXXV

Do you do these things, or do these things do you? It's the same old
question, as anything fits to cause all sorts of inevitabilities. Are you
having these thoughts or are these thoughts having you? I look over my
shoulder quickly and move on. Nature or nurture, possibly, though we all
say it's both. Richard L. Gross, I read at *The Bully Project*, says, "We are all
either bullies, bullied, or bystanders." But I've always thought there's at least
a fourth category, as all things wind down to something else that commences,
through many perilous situations, until the part winding down is your part
some night in the backyard looking at Saturn through a telescope. I've
always had a mole on my right earlobe, for instance, and so school afternoons
were long and tedious, how, when people single you out, and it's something
you can't change, you never really get away. My daughter Natalie, eleven
now, cried herself to sleep last night. You know? You don't get away
from that feeling. It lives with you, this unwelcome guest of yourself.

Not much new going on today, though. The play's titled *It Gets Better*,
and I guess it does, at least it's important we say that to the young,
so they don't despair. Say you have two apples in Act I, a red one
and a green one, and you know that in Act III, one of them has to go off.
The earth is slowing, my friends. The horses seem to go faster already.
We shall also endeavor to go faster, because that's how we're built.
Blame the watchmaker, not the watch, the watchmaker who would
probably just say something like, "These things interested me a great deal
for a time, but now they no longer do." And Kenton got food poisoning
from some bad tuna, but now he's all better. We saw Jeff outside in the sun,
sneezing. He said the sun's always made him do that. And Jamie
from across the street is outside sucking up leaves again with a mulching
machine that has a big hose on it. They're for her garden, which
is nearly an acre. It's all very practical, when anything could happen next,
and then it does. You hear the train sounds and the street sounds.
You're a bystander, or you're a witness, working on your empathy, as
Willie Nelson sings, "be careful what you're dreamin' or soon
your dreams'll be dreamin' you." Either way, the table of apples has fallen
over. Depending on the importance of your part, or the importance
of someone else's part that depends on your part, they rush to you,

just as leaves drop their trees, or that eighteen-wheeler I watched jackknife
down the highway once, like Disneyland. An E-ticket.

In my freshman year of high school, the seniors on the bus
wanted our names and Dunkin' Donuts. I told them I was Alfie Zindel,
and that I was allergic to donuts, thereby realizing that they didn't
have a very good plan for what to do next. They threw me in the bushes
when we got to school, which hurt a bit, but also made me laugh,
which was a bad idea. Keep your head down, they always say. So
they made me hold a stack of books over my head for the bus ride
home. And of course, I kept dropping them on their heads every time
we hit a bump. Mostly accidentally, I think now, but happily,
watching them getting hit over the head with it. Revenge is not subtle.
And I apologized, of course, being polite. Brains over brawn, they say,
but it would be better if you could have both. The future would be
much easier that way. And also if the good guys got the white hats,
sure, which is how we can tell they're the good guys, and if the bad guys
would just be bad guys, without a back story, and they're here so that you
can have your narrative arc. John Wayne is on his horse at the edge
of the clearing, facing four of them. He holds the reins in his teeth.
A pistol in one hand, rifle in the other, and he charges.

XXXVI

What year, what moment was it, when all the television aerials
came down from our roofs? And now, the skyline
is getting all junked up with dangerous-looking post-apocalyptic
telephone polls that list with hanging wires. You see them a lot
alongside railroad tracks. Depending on what song is playing
as we pass, it can begin to look orchestrated, some illustration
of our departure into decay. Cue the zombies or the apes
and go out abroad into the fields again.

"The future is a line of trees." I like saying things like that,
something kind of smoky and getting out around the edges
of whatever one might want to pin it to. But isn't that, itself,
a good description of the future? Or the *post*-future, I suppose,
as we got to the future quite a while ago now. Sometime
in the 60s, I think? When everything started happening
at the same time . . . only to end up
where all the telephone booths and tape decks ended up.

My father would take the TV up on the roof with him,
so that he could get the antenna positioned just so.
He quickly tired of having us help him. The endless calling out,
"How is it now?" and "Now try Channel 13!" which led invariably
to irritation when he'd come down and try the TV himself.
So there he was: Birmingham, Alabama, January 1976,
up on the roof with his beige/gray jacket, the TV balanced
on a pile of blankets in front of him, the aerial
between them, riding the house, his arms up to the sky.

XXXVII

I think "getting out of the way" is a great way to be helpful
to most people most of the time, especially
when I meet one of those people who reminds me
of the truth behind "killing someone
with kindness." And so we're all, no matter what, trapped
in our own heads, of course, and there's usually nothing different
about the day you started, it was the day you started,
that's all. What that has to do with being overly helpful, I'm not sure,
it just kind of came to me. Maybe it's just that it's all
some version of the unknown, and getting out of the way
seems an idea that assumes the least about other people.

It's good, I think, to assume as little as possible at all times. I had that
"ass of you and me" thing drilled into my brain
early on. Now, though, I find that you really can tell a lot about a book
by its cover. Currently I'm wearing a brown belt
with sneakers, and thinking, as I was always taught,
that sneakers aren't meant for outfits that require belts. Maybe we're all
right or all wrong or these distinctions are insignificant
over time. But isn't this just the sort of thing
people from the future will be seriously researching?

The book *I'm OK, You're OK* was floating around the house
when I was a kid. It was the 1970s, you know? The author, Thomas Harris,
postulates that the brain records past experiences
like a tape recorder, and keeping to the simple math, comes up with four
"life positions" that each of us may take. The four positions are: 1.
I'm Not OK, You're OK; 2. I'm Not OK, You're Not OK; 3.
I'm OK, You're Not OK; 4. I'm OK, You're OK.
It's a dumb idea, most likely, but that's probably fine too,
because if you take a dumb idea far enough,
it could touch glory. You never know. And sitting here,
as we mostly do, talking about all the people
we know, we're just census takers. We have these forms to fill out.

XXXVIII

Wherever I get to, someone's there. It's a busy place,
wherever we are. George Oppen calls it the "shipwreck
of the singular," if I'm reading him correctly,
though the day after "everything happening at once"
which was in the air back then, we find ourselves
making the same breakfast as before, and the windows still work
in the old way. There's always this lag-time between the first
serious relationship I was in, and every relationship
I've ever been in, with all our faces layering over the top
of ourselves, a love that is hopeless and waiting at your door.
Winnie Cooper, where are you now? Right?

We could ask ourselves such questions with impunity
in the past, but now, as information is cheap, these things
usually get answered within seconds, complete
with a picture surrounded by balloons and favorite inspirational
kitten. And when they don't get answered? Even now
things have a nasty habit of disappearing. The high school
I went to, I just found out recently, no longer
exists. The building is there on Wolf Hill Road, but it's now,
I think, called Saint Anthony's. So exits Holy Family, stage left,
pursued by bear. I suddenly feel a sense of loss,
even though I've been to none of the reunions.

You're right, you know, when you're seventeen. You're right
about it all, as I heard in "Powderfinger" for the first time
in the school cafeteria, lunch period, 1980, and "Rock Lobster"
at all the dances in that same cafeteria. But I hated
dances. I dislike large public gatherings of any sort. All these faces
looking around. The mysterious needs and desires—the
unknowability. How easy it is to criticize each other. I can
see them now in their purity, their unfettered beauty,
saying here he is, "thinking" again . . . and all these thoughts
seem so minor afterward. Where's the reach,
the achievement. Maybe it's better for both of us

this way. No, it's not you, it's me. Maybe we can still be friends. There's a company of wolves at the door, asking for you. Should I show them in?

XXXIX

"And every one of us, a kitten up a tree." It's a line
from the song "Born a Man," by Clem Snide, and it's
playing right now as I'm driving to work. So are we kittens?
Sometimes it seems so, the way we're all a little scared of the dark
now and then and we have all these movies to prove it. And only
fools rush in. Which I was once (at least), in Texas, in the fall,
in one of those Texas floods that Stevie Ray Vaughan
went on so about. There are other ways to think about it, I guess,
how usually we're less fools rushing in than we're just kind of
not really thinking much at all. It's the psychological variant
of Newton's first law of motion, how we move at a constant velocity
unless acted upon by an external force.

I should have thought more about external forces, or taken the radio
more seriously, but back then I wasn't aware of how much
force there is in piles of water, or what those poles
in dips of the road with measurements on them are for. So,
mistake one, I drove my Toyota Starlet into the low water crossing,
thinking it wasn't going to be very deep. When the engine
chugged, I backed out real quick, just before
it died. I left the car parked there and, mistake two, decided
to continue on foot. If I decided anything, really. Mostly,
I think I just kind of continued on. I made two steps. The third
never landed, instead, I found myself about twenty yards
down the runoff, holding onto some scrub trees, almost waterskiing
behind them, which has more to do with Newton's second law, I think, how
the acceleration of a body is directly proportional to, and in the same
direction as, the net force acting on the body,
and inversely proportional to its mass.

And that's pretty much the way I've done things since. Find myself
in a flood, check, and then having the thought of "now would be a good time
for a thought." The thought this time was to let go and swim
like mad. It's the only time I've ever gone swimming wearing work boots
and a leather jacket. I aimed for the shore, measuring the speed

of the water, some version of Newton's third law, and ended up getting into some brush another fifty yards or so downstream. What an amazing thing, to actually get to the bank. What an amazing thing, to stand up. What an amazing thing.

XL

Four of us are here at the moment. Will this
be a lasting memory to any
or all of us? The idea that "something
always happens" that we keep trotting out,
quickly falls apart as we then might ask ourselves
what happened each of the days of the last
week. This is section XL of my long poem, and so I've decided it's got to be the Extra Large
section then, maybe with really, really long lines or something. How, in the past we
had Small, Medium, and Large, and then we found that just wouldn't do for a
growing country, so we added XL, and then XXL, and on. Well, there you
go. My spellchecker didn't recognize XXL, just then (2009), but, when
looking at this again (2013), suddenly spellchecker is just fine with it.
What does this mean? Will rosy-cheeked angels descend to bring
an XXL gift to us all? Shouldn't there be a party or something?
Some brilliance? Bright colors? Maybe they'll tell us stories
of UHF and VHF, how things are always something else

suddenly. And when something big does happen, how will we react? That's
one of those questions I've heard veterans or those who've survived
some terrible ordeal talk about. The kidnapped, the shot, how now,
for them, it's no longer a question. They know. They just know. It's a gift
one gets through adverse circumstances, this thing all wrapped up
and delivered through pain and loss, as an event in time.

We're planning a trip to Chicago for Thanksgiving, which is in a couple weeks,
and that reminds me that last year, driving up I-35, just before the Iowa border,
there was sudden snow and a multi-car accident right in front of us. A flash
of double red brake lights from all the cars around us, and the next thing I knew
I was driving on the median and then back onto the highway that was deserted
but for us and snow. I thought I'd never forget what song was playing
on the car stereo, but now I've forgotten. I'll pretend it was something
by Woody Guthrie, which I know it wasn't, and maybe it went,
"We are ramblers so they say, / We are only here today."

XLI

If only you could burn memories in a little pile
and bring whiskey and marshmallows. It would be
nice. And it's the basis for a lot of stories and
songs. One time, in Athens, Ohio, we all went out
to what we called "The Bish," which was a house
where several guys lived. It had some woods and a lot of
empty space. It was late, we had a fire going, where Eric
had decided to burn some books, and maybe some
of his papers from classes. I think there was
some desire to ceremoniously burn a large dictionary,
as well. One of those 1950 editions of Merriam-Webster
that seem to be everywhere, with guitars and alcohol.
And then James came out with his trumpet.

Things get confused after that, we say. A couple months ago
things got confused when my mother-in-law was walking
with two of her dogs as one of them, the larger one (a Springer),
decided to kill the smaller one (a Jack Russell). I thought
I could just reach into the Springer's mouth and make her drop
the Jack Russell. Turns out, it doesn't work that way
when a dog decides to kill another dog. We got the two apart,
and the Jack Russell lived. But I've also got this scar now
on my right middle finger, and I've lost most of my nail.
The bite was deep. The fingertip was numb for several weeks.

We tell stories constantly, usually for no reason
other than to say we've all lived and we're
still here, which is why I have such a difficult time
with them. We're not always still here. My uncle
rolled a tractor over on himself while mowing
a hillside, and was impaled on the gear shift. It was
on his land. A place he'd been mowing
for years. And when the story is over, we'll start
telling it again. It will be no different, the way
my mother tells it every few minutes, in what's

becoming more and more her eternal present,
unaware that she's just told it, because it's
comforting to be in a story, as all stories
are autobiography in a landscape, and the landscape
goes on all night, dotted with little fires.

XLII

I changed my mind. I was going to stop writing this poem, but now
I'm not, because I heard someone say, in the hallway earlier,
that she had changed her mind, and it seemed a lovely idea, the way
it struck me, to "change one's mind." I'd like to do that. Presto
Change-O. We decide with our attention what has meaning
and what doesn't. So now, continuing is what has meaning,
and how Natalie's telling me a story while I'm sitting here, deciding
to keep writing this, about an alternative to the Santa story, as we're
getting near Christmas, where a girl flies around giving presents. She
likes her story better, as she's a girl, and the idea of flying is such
a good one. We all have these dreams where we fly. Looking up
"flying dreams" just now, I'm asked the question, "If you have
a flying dream, ask yourself what you're flying over." And that,
it goes on to say, will lead you to what the dream means. "See
the gate agent," as they say. And then, "WARNING:
the gates are closing and will not open again."

It's final stuff, as Neko Case has it, that heaven will smell like an
airport. And how they call them "terminals." I saw a picture
of farmland and trees taken from the air recently, and it resembled
sheet music how they spread out in lines. I had an idea, looking down,
that we're living across a large score. Flights of fancy, a trill, to the latest
brilliance of the waves. And to continue the thought, as I'm interested
in continuing thoughts, often, when I'm flying, and sitting between
the engines, I swear I can hear music, sometimes quite loud, orchestral
and oscillating. I've heard other people can hear that as well. So it's not
just me. Sometimes I can hear it in the pipes when I'm in the shower
as well. It's beautiful, flying, looking down. Last winter, I flew
from Austin to San Francisco, and for most of the way the 737 kept
fairly low. Low enough to pick out cars. It reminded me of being a kid,
and all those dreams where I'd get to reach down and pick cars up,
and draw new rivers with my finger. My father was a pilot. I loved
flying with him, and I went every time I had the chance. It was always
small planes, and we kept low over the fantasy towns of the west,

the one-stops, single-lights, under a sky that's always blue, in the day,
and at night the lights were in squares and stars, and never to be finished.

What's not to love about this world then?

XLIII

What Social Security means to me is that if I continue working
until the age of seventy, my monthly payment would be about
$2,090. At some point we all have the moment, for me
it was this one, of standing there knowing the world
will be over. "You take your movie
to a new town, said the street on fire," as they say. A feeling
of security *doesn't* rise, seeing my benefits
estimated. I picture us there before the fish tank. "Speak up,
the fish can't hear you," you say. It's never
convincing, is it? Telling them they're dust and to dust
they shall return? I was talking to Paul's wife
the other day, and she was saying he's going to go another year,
and then decide if he's going to retire. She's
not sure he will. "It's all he's ever done," she says. "And
I've no idea what he'd do all day with me going
to work." Some actual things creep in, like Germans
in the 1930s. Formulas and stratagems. And suddenly
you're seventy. Your father's a tourist now, in some other place.

What are the odds, do you think? "Your name is
no accident," the advertisement reads. It goes on: "Numbers
govern much, if not *most* of what happens in your life,
relationships, and finances." So there you are. From
K. calling to say the divorce is coming through,
to Brendan's brother drowning twenty-five years ago . . . "Life, our /
Life anyway, is between," John Ashbery says
in "Daffy Duck in Hollywood," the in-betweenest of all places.

Moments seem to always be doing that, though
the mimetic fashions change, and we come in and out
of relevance to the advancing narrative, even
as it's ours, we think, and imagine ourselves at the award show,
thanking the little people. We're thanking ourselves,
then. It reminds me of a show I was listening to a few weeks back,
about the Royal Shakespeare Company, how the question

was about realism, how we think now that we're in a more
realistic age, but how all ages maybe think that
about themselves, it's not that acting changes, but that the
communally agreed-upon reality changes. Well,
there's something, I guess, in a time of displacement,
finding myself somewhere I was unaware of.

XLIV

"Is our ability to have confidence in another owing more to others
or to ourselves?" Now we're getting somewhere. When I worked
at a restaurant, back in that first year of Social Security
deductions, it always seemed to be back of the house vs.
front of the house. I think we all liked it that way. Later,
when we ended up at the same parties, we didn't seem to
mind each other. One of the waiters told me, once, that he had a vision
when he was a teenager, and then one day, he suddenly
couldn't remember what it was. Nothing was left. He'd lost confidence
in it or in himself or something. Like waking from a dream. He
described it that way. Like waking, and whether or not we like it,
we're all waking in a Buddhist, non-knowing stance,
in regards to most things.

When I was about ten, I was served
with divorce papers by a sheriff, in uniform. It was a mistake, of course,
and he was apologetic, but still I should have taken it
as a sign. Two or so years later, I forget, but it was when
we were living on Long Island, I had a Penny Saver route. In some places,
they're called Greensheets, I think? Or Penny Press? I was on my route,
and had just thrown to a fourplex, when a man came out,
he must have been about sixty, and said he hadn't gotten his Penny Saver
in the past, and wanted to talk about it. So I followed him
into his apartment. Once I was inside, he shut the door
behind me. The walls were covered in pornography. He turned to me
and said, "I just want to dance."

He didn't do much. Held me close. Kept his hands
to my backside, all over my back and into my pants. But there
was no music. All the music was in his head, and I was able to get out
after just a minute or two. Nothing worse. And the punch line
is that when I was a safe distance away, I turned and saw him
in his door, and asked him if he really had a problem
with his Penny Saver or not. It would mean my job. One of these days
they're going to come up with an application

that will have our emotions for us, and then things
will be perfect. All things will be perfected. All will be made trivial.

XLV

Life gives us numerous opportunities to practice counting. Five years.
Ten. Say you have three green apples, and Teri brings a basket of turnips
to the office, how many days are there left until Thanksgiving?
That sort of thing. "It's all one process." As Jasper Johns
said to John Cage sometime around 1963. And process
is a form of structure. And other things happen
gradually, in the way that mountains are very slow waves
or waves are very fast mountains. Either way, it's a process
which makes a structure. Geological time. I've seen the same thing said
about birdsong and whalesong. "It's all one song," as
Neil Young says on the *Broken Arrow* tour,
in reply to his own comment, "They all sound the same."

And then it's all one arrow, time's arrow, and all things have their
return: the uncanny, or fashion, or what-have-you. So we count. My
three marriages. My fourteen days of vacation. And one of the times
things come back, they come back as farce, though we're never told
which time. It a grab-bag of possibilities. I thought about that
last month at the school fair, where my kids played the fishing game,
with sticks and string and a wooden clip, whatever those wooden clips
are called, and someone behind the cardboard wall attached
an elastic alien or google-glasses, then pulled three times . . .
Robin's aunt and uncle were in the middle of their divorce
when she moved back in. Promises are made. And now he has
a new kidney that he got from Carla, another of Robin's aunts,
who's completed her round of chemotherapy, and is back home.

At some point, though, people and things stay gone. There are
telephone calls, sure. Sometimes court proceedings. An evening
or two of why did we get together and why did we part,
and then another parting. And one of them is farce.
Maybe it was that time Person X showed up at my apartment
in San Marcos, Texas, at night, in the rain, wearing a raincoat and heels,
and nothing else. And now, fifteen years on, it's coming on Christmas:
short days, colored lights. We're time machines, physics tells us,

and there are many ways to travel, but only one direction. Consider the possibilities. It's soccer night. Tomorrow, a meeting. We'll need to pick something up for dinner on the way home.

XLVI

Answer the question with a Yes or No. Indeed. Because
that's how life works, right? Yes or no, up or down, with me
or against me. Good person. Bad person. Bad dog. "I've been
a bad, bad boy." Lou Costello's tag line. "One can even set up
quite ridiculous cases." Schrödinger writes, "A cat is penned up
in a steel chamber, along with . . . a Geiger counter, there is
a tiny bit of radioactive substance, so small that perhaps
in the course of the hour, one of the atoms decays, but also,
with equal probability, perhaps none; if it happens, the counter tube
discharges, and through a relay releases a hammer that shatters
a small flask of hydrocyanic acid. If one has left this entire system
to itself for an hour, one would say that the cat still lives
if meanwhile no atom has decayed. The psi-function of the entire system
would express this by having in it the living and dead cat
(pardon the expression) mixed or smeared out in equal parts."

Doing an image search on "Schrödinger's Cat" yields mostly comics.
My favorite of the few I looked at had this for a caption: "Schrödinger
was arrested for cruelty to animals. His fate is uncertain." Is this
a realistic way to imagine fate? To be alive and dead, smeared out
in a psi-function? I've met a few people who make me think perhaps
he's onto something. And what about close calls? The tree that fell on me
at my uncle's farm the year before he died, fell with me perfectly
in the center of the V the huge limbs made. "Missed it by that much."
Maxwell Smart's tag line. It was Chaplinesque. And the time I was pushed
off an eight-foot wall at a birthday party in the fourth grade, landing
on the top of my head, which, thinking about it now,
could have been serious, but only left me with a headache.

My mother's father died on Christmas Day when she was three. My
first father died in a car accident on the Fourth of July when I was
three. How does the old joke go? "Other than that, Mrs. Lincoln,
how was the play?" An atom of a substance decays and the cat
is dead. An atom of a substance remains intact and the cat lives.

XLVII

Where's the fun in doing something you've done a million times? Well,
maybe it's not what someone else has done, and they like watching you.
It could be considered a service. Maybe you teach them. They say
there's no higher calling, or almost no higher calling, depending on how
one feels about callings. The football coach had a calling to coach
this team, it was his life dream, and he was the coach for three months
until he died last week while mowing his lawn, and now today they're
having a Celebration of Life service for him at the stadium. He was
forty-nine. There will be a public viewing in an hour at the Ron Houston
Performing Arts center. I could make it if I left right now.

It all depends on where you think you're going, as we say we're going
somewhere, but we also say there's nowhere really to get to
but in your head—which is a comfort only the safe can explore. I was
in baseball for a year, for example, standing in the outfield wondering
what I was doing there, watching the grass. Once, I was stung by a bee
in the fourth inning. After games, I'd get a Mr. Pibb. Birmingham,
Alabama. Summer, 1977. "Who is this person?" we ask, looking at pictures
of ourselves outside the premiere of *Star Wars*. It's a good question.
A fine question. It's "Pick Your Skill" day, and we go around the room,
another version of "What Super Hero Would You Be." Eliot chooses
Anything Boy, and Natalie chooses "I Don't Know." I choose falling
out of trees. The last time I did that, I landed at Robin's feet
with the air knocked out of me, and I couldn't breathe or talk
for a second or so. And then I could. It makes a pattern.

As for getting somewhere, I just walked around the office with my eyes closed
and did a pretty fair job of it. Typing was kind of a mess though. I thought
it would have been the other way around. It's everywhere around you,
as in those old Palmolive commercials where Madge says, "You're
soaking in it." She did a lot of those commercials, from 1966 to 1992.
He name was Jan Miner, and in France her character was named Françoise.
In Germany, Switzerland, and Austria she was Tilly, and in Finland
she was Marissa. For some reason that means something to me right now.
I just looked it up, and found she died on February 18th, 2004. She was eighty-six.

XLVIII

What is the reason for harboring ill-will toward another?
What is the reason for forgiving them? There are so many examples
with a ruler and the color gray. Who do I have to forgive?
Who has to forgive me? I hate that. I hate this whole topic.
What am I supposed to say next? Start confessing something? Why?
What good do such things ever do? I'm more understanding
of someone who says, "I'm taking my confessions with me." Good.
As long as they're the garden-variety confessions. The "say three Hail Marys
and apologize to _____" confessions. Because confession
is supposed to lead to something. We're changed, right? Brand new
soul, the way the archaic torso of Apollo makes us also want to change
our lives, only we never do. Or else, yes, of course we do, but only
for the time it takes to get to the parking lot. "Man, it's all been
forgiven," as The National have it, "The swans are a-swimmin'." And
they continue, "I'll explain everything to the geeks." Sounds good to me.

Amanda reminded me yesterday that I used to, a couple years ago,
make declarations that I was continually new, John II, and then John III,
always a new model. Always turning a corner. Neither of us
could remember where I left off or when. What John am I up to now?
Maybe XLVIII? Agents of change, we order "The Regular," as change
is a version of "What has this meant to you?" It's Neil Young's birthday today,
November XII, MMIX. He's LXIV, XX years older than I am
(and what a mess Roman numerals make of these things). Happy Birthday,
then, Neil: what has this meant to you? And Happy Birthday
to everyone else, while I'm at it, because Happy Birthday is good. Happy Birthday
to the singular and collective, the way birthday parties sum things up:

My mother (this was years ago) bakes a cake, and takes it to the party, and
there's this tension between them (is this my memory, or is it a story
I was told?). Call her Person A. And so Person B extends her hands
to receive the cake at the door as my mother releases her grip. The cake
(did you see this coming?) falls to the ground between them. *Woosh*.

XLIX

The college mascot is visiting the elementary school. It's
celebrity reading day, and it strikes me as suddenly funny,
as mascots are mute creatures best experienced
from a distance. Last week the university president
was the celebrity reader. He read a book called *T
Is for Turkey*. I asked Robin if it was an autobiography.

I love it when life gives us these little punch lines. Like the way
"that's what *she* said," keeps making the rounds, which was once,
apparently "Said the actress to the bishop," which comes from
Britain, and might date from Elizabethan times, or, the much better,
to some at least, when someone says something with an "-er" ending
to you, you can reply, "but you brought her." Soccer? You
brought her. Sucker? You get the drift. Hold a screw in your palm,
and ask someone if they wanna screw. If someone is wearing something
with a heart on it, you can say, "I see you've got a heart on."
(That one doesn't work well on paper.)

One of the ones I've known for a long time, I picked up
from a guy in high school, Vick Vanucci: pick up a leaf
and then hand it to someone, saying, "leaf me alone." A couple months
after I heard him say that, I got to use a similar one on him. He was flipping
my social studies book closed while I was trying to read (it was
reading aloud day in social studies class), and writing "YOU ARE A
DI_K" on the inside heal of my sneakers that were under my desk
for gym class next period. I'd had enough. So I waited my chance
and then hit him as hard as I could across the back of his trumpet playing hand
with my gym lock. It was a dial combination lock
with a big circular knob on the front. There was already swelling
by the end of class. So then, next period, there we were
in the gym. He does the whole arm-up-behind-my-back-smashing-my-face-
into-the-lockers thing. Ah, high school. He said, "Tell everybody
you're a dick!" And I replied, "OK, you're a dick."
I sometimes think it was the greatest moment of my life.

L

"L" for landscape, where all of us are having different
experiences right now. What is there to do but wave
and say, "Hi"? So "Hi" then, from my little scrap
of the Midwest, where I'm, nearly always, contentedly
filled with non-belief, or maybe un-belief. But not
disbelief. It seems to me that disbelief is a joining into an economy
of the conversation, and it gives me the feeling
that one is being incredulous, and I don't feel
incredulous. There are so many things not to believe in,
and John Lennon, back around 1970, made a point of it
on the *John Lennon/Plastic Ono Band* album, singing, "I don't believe
in Zimmerman" and then "I don't believe in Gita" and building up
to "I don't believe in Beatles." (My spellcheck recognizes "Beatles"
but not "Gita." Should I be worried?) The song's called
"God." And maybe the whole thing for me stems
from my terrible problem with authority. And how authority figures
always seem to be able to tell. Traffic Police, mostly.

On Monday, I made the mistake of opening my car door
while a local cop was writing me a ticket
for having expired tags. He told me that sort of thing
would get me "taken down" in a city, and I was lucky
we're more relaxed in a small town like
Maryville. I thanked him for not
taking me down. My kids were interested in what
"taking down" meant. I said it meant we're all in this together.

A state trooper in Texas once, late at night, asked me on the highway,
after pulling me over, if I wanted to take a swing at him maybe,
man to man. Or the guy who, in jogging shorts at around three
in the morning a couple years later, asked me what I was doing
in an apartment complex while I was delivering newspapers,
and I said, "Well, what are you doing?" And he said, "Uh-uh,"
as he pulled a gun on me, and then a badge from his other
pocket as the idea of duration rose up around us

like a beautiful crystal presence. I could feel the air
in my blood, the blood in my heart. My desire to be a part
of the future, where my biggest hope for an afterlife
is that it would be like the AARP fantasy of retirement,
where we're all smiling tourists going places and
solving mysteries. I'll be able to fly, as well, and go faster
than the speed of light, as I have this recurring desire
to fly out past the planets. Maybe find a place with rock candy
mountains, and someone there
with a clipboard of answers to questions
such as, "Whatever happened to Rosie Perez?" And,
"Who stole that money from the restaurant
back in 1985, and how did they do it?"

LI

"Be proud of who you are
and what you want to be!" is the slogan that won
a contest on CNN, I heard this morning. Apparently
it was a self-esteem contest, one that's going to do wonders for our prison
population. And then comes some actual
news: Water was found on the moon,
scientists say. The discovery came out of a mission
a month ago in which a satellite hit into a crater
near the lunar south pole. "Welcome to the future!

We're glad you made it!" As Firesign Theatre
said in the distant past. And now, they still teach children
to write in cursive. Why? Where do we go from here? First,
where is *here*? And second, how will we be traveling? And third,
will it just be used as a metaphor for something? There's
a resounding chorus of "Dance cowboy," and then
the shooting starts. Or else it's a rousing chorus
of "We don't need no stinkin' badges," and then
the shooting starts. Either way,
the shooting starts. Sarah's father died when
she was thirteen, so in some respect, she'll be thirteen
for the rest of her life, and he'll be driving her home, lecturing her
about her grades and the importance of applying herself.

It's another of those occasions when you're speaking
and someone interrupts you to ask what you're talking about,
and then you have to, what? Go where? It's a long row
of first times. It will always be so. Whenever someone
would ask my father what time it was, he'd tell them
how to build a watch. That's the joke I used to use. Don't give
someone a fish, teach them how to fish. They'll know what time it is
forever. It's 2:32 in the afternoon right now. Friday
the 13th. The new moon's waning. Black tambourine.

LII

None of these things is ever quite it. In much
the way that all intention is at odds
with other intention. The theme of most lives
is *AAAAAH*, and there we are. It makes
for very short reports. They were all in agreement
that it was going to be chilly yesterday,
and then it was quite warm actually. We emerged
from our buildings, shedding our jackets
like the final scene of some liberation movie, *Logan's Run*,
maybe. We don't need these coverings anymore. Life,
my friends, is new. And we will face it newly divested.

"Make your mark," they say to us, and then they say, "Leave
no traces." Granted, these are for different situations,
but still, the leaving of marks/traces is the point, and that
makes sense. We want to feel that our lives
have meaning, and the easiest way to ascertain meaning
is to look behind one for signs of having been
there. The legacy starts now. The boy's named
Junior, and we're off. What buildings will have our names
on them. What bridges. Initiatives. What destiny
lays us over the top of our mortality. Our great
contributions line our shelves striking poses,
saying "Go West, my boy!" and "Plastics!" My father
wanted me to be a lawyer, since it was obvious
I wasn't going to be a priest. He always wanted
to be a priest. He used to invent things when he was
younger, one was an artificial horizon for the dashboard
of small planes, but then technology came along
and he's asking me questions like, "But where is
the Internet?" He made great pinewood derby cars.

And equally, when one is out and about in the woods
or perhaps in an affair at work, one wants to leave nothing
disturbed, to leave the place just as you found it

for someone else to experience later,
as if for the first time. Everyone thanks you,
and it's everyone's birthday, and you get to keep
nothing but the pictures and your private thoughts.

LIII

"Have you had a good life?" Good question. In the grand scheme
of things, we're all fairly equal. We just travel in varying degrees
of comfort. There's a rhythm to a life, they say, like
the seasons. "What walks on four legs then two then three . . ." goes
the riddle, but the rhythm of the seasons works best if you speed them up
really fast. Errors too, like Eros, are a rhythm
only when speeded up. That's not true really, but it does
make the time go by faster. Another thought is that the stock market
is like DNA, and its need to replicate causes business
to transact. We, by and large, don't factor in. You can't
make an omelet without breaking eggs, as Ronald Reagan said once
as an explanation of his foreign policy. It finds a rhythm
or it doesn't, which nonetheless becomes its rhythm,
as another way to classify people. Happy. Unhappy.

When I was young, we moved every three years. You
could set your watch to it. It's been mostly convenient. "Mostly
harmless," as *The Hitchhiker's Guide to the Galaxy*
describes Earth, a place, where for most of us, most things
look like furniture. I'll scratch your back,
and you scratch mine. Things move along. I'm having this feeling,
coming back to this poem a year later,
November 16, 2010, Natalie's ninth birthday, that I'm
as happy as I've ever been. I brought one of Eliot's toys
to work today, a little stuffed blue creature that when you squeeze
its belly, its mouth moves and it says differing versions of "Eeep."

Big. Little. Would you rather look through a telescope
or a microscope? That seems an interesting way to classify people,
but perhaps everyone would say "telescope," as currently
that's what I'd say, so I imagine perhaps everyone would,
as I keep getting little reminders that I'm average. But being average
is rather special in its way too, as one could then be considered
emblematic, a thing to hold up as what we are, a kind of clairvoyance,
standing in a field of corn, the way all measurements are general.

The more precisely you measure—a coastline, for instance—the longer the distance becomes. A precise measurement of any coastline, they say, then, is infinite. Lucky us.

LIV

Where's the line between what constitutes repetition
and what constitutes change? Right now I'm thinking forgetfulness
is just as good as careful planning, similar to how doing nothing
is usually just as helpful as quick, decisive action. Chance
actions. John Cage made detailed plans on chance. Yesterday
Natalie was working on a catchphrase. That's something
to do while waiting. Mine would be something like, "What are we
talking about again?" Natalie didn't like that one, and went for,
"Oh *yeah*," I think. I'm terrible at remembering such things.

That's been my problem with nicknames, as well. I always
wanted one, and for a while I was going to be Dutch,
I've always thought, and then, a few years ago I met a guy
whose nickname was Dutch, and as I was telling him Dutch
also used to be my nickname, I remembered that my nickname
used to be Danish. I almost spit my drink. It was
a job interview. What a thing to remember at a job interview. Well,
there you are. Maybe *that* should be my catchphrase, or maybe,
even better: "The sun's going to get really big and swallow the earth."
I imagine that could be a perfect caveat to most situations.

We're out on the lake. It's a beautiful day. For a moment, if you're not
thinking of anything, you can't be either shallow or deep. And then
you can say, "The sun's going to get really big
and swallow the earth." Ah, catchphrases. And if the you
at this point is Natalie, you could say, "Oh *yeah*,"
and there we'd be. And all the little ripples around
the boat. We couldn't live without them, how the universe seems
made for us, which is called the Anthropic principle, weak (WAP)
or strong (SAP), depending. Douglas Adams, in response,
used the metaphor of a living puddle examining its shape.
We are here, and we ripple, then, caught in a gravity well. And then
I hear there are some planets, called Untethered Planets
that orbit nothing at all. To which Natalie replied, "*Interesting*,"
as she does now, a few years later, 2012. Which,
according to Mayan eschatology, was or wasn't to be our last.

LV

Looking at each other just now, which is the intrusion:
the environment, as we're trying to talk, or us? It's worth
thinking about for a bit, how Morton Feldman
and John Cage were talking about it in 1966, the nature
of intrusion, where it comes from. There's always another way
to look at things (is that music or traffic?), which seems to me right now,
another way to support the idea that doing nothing
is the best course of action in most situations. Just sit tight.

Once, when I was in high school, six or so of us
went to Brendan's house for the weekend. His parents
were probably away. I think it was after their divorce,
and a couple years before his brother drowned. We got a case
of beer, and took it to a little park overlooking the Long
Island Sound, where we could wave at Connecticut. It was
night. It took almost no time at all for the police
to show up, the way they tend to do in these stories. I decided
the jig was up and just stayed sitting on the case of beer
resting beneath a little tree. Everyone else took off. Funny thing,
so did the police, giving chase. I still had a beer
in my hand, sitting there, watching them all run off
into the dark of the little woods. So I picked up
the case of beer and carried it back to Brendan's house to wait,
and then that becomes something of a study.

When I was young, I lived in Orange County and ended up
going to Disneyland thirty-five times. I was trapped at "Yo ho,
yo ho, a pirate's life for me" once, for about forty-five minutes. "Don't tell them,
Carlos" one of the townswomen kept saying. We're also music,
as our world is always coming to an end. We're relevant awhile,
and then it's some other currency with all the wrong faces on it,
and people are talking a language we've never heard before.
I keep thinking that if I just keep sitting here, I'll see us all come running back
out of the woods. Some turn of the dial. And we'll be numerous,
won't we, and we'll all matter, mostly harmless, sitting there

telling each other these stories, and each of us remembering it so that we're the one who gets away.

LVI

The landscape is on fire, and where are you
going to start? Everyone and everything
is burning. Are you a firefighter or a fire chief? Where
does the buck stop? It was my name on the deposit slip. The deposit
was for just under $3,000, and it was missing.
And $2,500 was missing from the safe as well. Then they
started dragging everything they could find
into it. I was divorced at twenty. I put a bunch of tape
on the side exit door so it wouldn't lock. The lie-detector
guy said my answers weren't very dependable, but weren't
damning either. So there I was in my own little detective show. Well,
the tape was an easy one. I put it there when the drive-thru speaker
wasn't working, and we had to keep running out and back,
and the door would lock behind us. It seemed a crisis
decision, so I didn't think to make a note about it. I was being a team
player. And the divorce, isn't that pretty much everyone's story?

Once, when I was nineteen, I had a job interview
with a Wall Street firm. I can't remember specifically
what the job was for. They just sat there on either side of me,
these two guys, asking things like, "Aren't you just
chasing your own death?" I think that interview
fundamentally changed something in me. Not only
didn't I want the job after that, but I also had a distinct
feeling that maybe it had never happened. Maybe it was a vision,
the last two cents I was going to get from the numinous.
The overcoat I was carrying didn't fit me. It was a prop. Something
to carry. Reality is a parade of people twisting and saying, "Boo"
as we're all chasing our own waiting rooms. Or something like that.

"We have it right here. You were the one who signed the deposit slip.
You can talk all you want, but you can't poke a hole in it,"
the district manager said to me from behind a massive mustache.
There I was in the office of a Carl's Jr. in San Antonio, Texas, 1985.
He handed the deposit slip to me, or more, pushed it in my direction. So

I looked at it. What else was I to do? I picked up a pencil
and poked a hole in it. Right beside my name. A little empty space.
A little empty space with lead all around the edges.

LVII

There are stories we don't tell, for whatever reason. Mostly
embarrassment, I'm thinking right now. Or,
more specifically, that then people wouldn't like me,
or would have some conception of me that I
don't want them to have, accurate or not. So I'm feeling today
that, as I'm being non-fictional and truthful,
or at least because I'm forcing myself
to write without making anything up,
that I should at least nod to all the stories
I'm not telling.
Because that would be telling, wouldn't it?

A moment of silence then
where my stories that are not being told
can mingle with yours. Let's drive across the state.
Let's go over the river. Let's run off
into the woods with them. And what is a life anyway
if not partially hidden? Is any of this a life? And what of the stories
we *would* tell, but we forget? Like the time I just remembered
when I fell backward into an empty fish tank
that was lying on its side, breaking out the glass,
wedging myself into the jagged edges. When I pulled myself out
I could feel the blood going down my legs, but
I couldn't see it. No one was home. I was
a teenager. By the time I got to our neighbor's house (who
was a cop), I was woozy with
thinking about it. And I haven't thought about it since. It all blends
into the soup of our inner lives . . .

The only time I ever went to a psychoanalyst
was because there was this free consultation offer. The only thing he said,
at the end of the forty-five minutes, was that
I had a lot of stuff we could work on. There you are. And so what
do we do with them, these stories we don't tell? I admit
that I have few answers, if any. I got a tattoo once. I'd do it again,

even though I nearly fainted. I'm not much good with needles.
Most all of these things we've done, if the circumstances
were right, we'd do again, I've heard. So thank you.
It feels good to get that off my chest.

LVIII

Richard's back, talking about *Easy Riders and Raging Bulls*,
a documentary of the auteur period
in American film, and how it closes with the shot from the end
of *Raging Bull*, where De Niro's face is hamburger
and he says, "You never got me down." I'm struck,
now that he's left, how we all cling to ways of doing things
because they tell us where we are, or where we were
when we were our most happy, like I've heard we do
with hairstyles. I don't know if I really
believe that, but there is a way that we cling to things
long after we should've stopped. What is it
that makes us do that? And then we pretend it's a virtue.

Maybe I'm doing it now. That's one
of my greatest fears, that I'll wake up one morning
and realize I've been clinging to something that's long gone,
and now we're both ghosts. But then there's this other
story, the story of perseverance. We all want to be *that*
person, the one who keeps going, who at long last
is shown to have been right all along. The way they say
honesty is a virtue. But still there's as much weight put on playing
by their rules, where in Rome, you say yes to the toga.

In fourth grade, maybe third, several of us were passing
back and forth a paper on which we were writing
every bad word we could think up. The usual words, yes,
but including such flights of fancy as "Flesh Gordon"
and "Mike Hunt." When we were inevitably caught,
we told the teacher that Danny Mendola, the student
who tormented us at recess, our bully, Danny, gave it to us.

LIX

Most things aren't necessary. So? Are we to impoverish ourselves
to make the point? And to whom are we making it? We all
go our various ways after high school, separated into what Nancy calls
"money attractors" and "money repellers." A couple decades
later, we check in, most of us. First, when we're
around thirty-eight, and then, after that, whenever. Vick is a lawyer
and raises dogs, and has written a book on cops and has
been on TV (attractor). Brendan's in a band, still, between
Kansas City and various points in Colorado (repeller).
My brother's in Chicago, working for Kraft (attractor). Jackie
is still in New York, as is most everyone else I knew then . . .

If we could sit in several places at once, as our particles
are apparently able to do, I'm thinking right now, we'd know
better how to communicate with each other. Some
better version of waving as we pass on our way to find our box
of rain checks. What if we were to list them, our rain checks,
and find the ones to cash? This time it's, "Yes,
I'll do that! I'll go!" How different would any of us
be? Or are we destined to be what we are? "You gotta
have faith," George Michael sang, but mostly faith
is a wind that blows from all directions at once.

I remember Watergate as bored looking men on TV
preempting reruns of *Voyage to the Bottom of the Sea*. We were between
houses at the time, staying in an apartment, where the landlady
had a granddaughter whom she wanted to have play with me, but not
my brother. We both kind of knew why, but not enough to say—
especially then, when none of us, including him, knew exactly
what race he was. He's always ignored it, and I've
always been a little jealous, which is another trick of adoption.
I also remember gluing a Popsicle stick to my upper lip,
as a mustache. It burned. And now I'm reading that we all
have invisible lives that encircle us, some imagined thing that defines us
in some way, and I'm thinking it's more true to think that there's nothing

invisible about us. This is what we are. Look around. We stagger because we stagger. It's where we get to.

LX

Improving our circumstances has been a stalled idea
for some time now. I grew up in the era of domes
and visions and the imminent arrival of
a new world, and instead we got the 1980s. John Cage
once proposed a Summit Lecture Series
on War, where all the national leaders would individually
address the world on why it's important
we kill people. It was a great critique until
they realized he was serious, that he thought there
might be something to know, something
to find out, which is why, I suppose, it's the
academics and artists who are always the first to go.

World betterment—even saying it sounds like
an advertisement for sometime around 1968, where
the women might still come and go, conceivably
talking of Michelangelo. Michael and Richard
were talking about that couplet of T. S. Eliot's this afternoon,
how it's being thought about again in the introduction
to a new anthology, and for a second I remembered
an idea I had one time of how each of us has
internal and external lives behind two different walls,
like the interior and exterior of a hat, and that
no one can ever see both at the same time, unless
one were to spin the hat on its brim, forming a blurry oval.

That probably doesn't connect to anything, I'm thinking
right now, a few hours later. But *Bob the Builder* is playing
on the TV, and my son's watching it, and he's named
Eliot with the "E-L-I-O-T" spelling. Bob has just dropped
his construction helmet, and I thought how
they're able to build whatever future they want on TV,
which is another reason not to like it, the way artists
are often not liked for their alternate worlds, as the universe
constantly contains everything in it, so that no matter
how big or how small it is, it's always the same size.

LXI

I want a house with a lot of windows, and all the windows
stained glass. And to live in a place
with a lot of sun. Piles and piles of sun. Last night
the TV went to static, and Natalie, one day
past her eighth birthday, said, "I LOVE
this channel!" and then we spent a few minutes
making things up about trucks and people
playing in the park, and I mentioned my house
on the hill with stained glass. Eliot, still three, said
he could see it, and that it looked red.

Twenty years ago I was living with a woman
who had a son, about three. We lived in a trailer park,
and I had to pick up food for them
from the Baptist church food bank. She was
too embarrassed, she said. I've heard she lives
in Alabama now, and works for the postal service. Back then
one could still work on cars. These days it's all
indicator lights and schematics. But back then,
I spent a little time every Saturday putting more
bailing wire around the drive train.

The house I'm living in now has a lot of windows,
but not many on the west side, which would look
great through stained glass. I have one stained-glass star
in the west side, in a little window over our stairwell.
When the light hits it just right,
I like to stand in it for a moment.
"The sun is full of candy," Natalie said yesterday.
She knows better, she's studied the sun in school,
but we're both happier this way, making these things
real, because someday we won't be.

LXII

Is your life the series of events
or is it something else? Maybe this is another of those
"are you a dog person or a cat person" kind of things—
but I've always been dogged by the whole "sins of the heart"
and "state of grace" economy on one side, and the
"fake it 'till you make it" on the other. I'm sorry. I mean it.
I feel this need to apologize, but I'm going to have to side
with the exterior on this one, walking by the houses, seeing the people
walking in and out. First warm day after a series
of cold days. Guessing at intentions and inner lives
has always left me standing on train platforms late at night,
in winter, inappropriately dressed.

Looking at us this way, then, the "keep your enemies closer" thing
would seem to be the logic behind most marriages,
and most of everything else as well. We're in our cars,
and it reminds me of driving a guy from work to his AA meeting,
1987 or 8—or maybe it was his NA meeting—because I promised
I would, and they kind of brought me into it, and I felt too something,
not really embarrassed, but I didn't want to seem
like I was trying to look superior or aloof, so I went along with it—
I even went back a second time when the guy
whose name I don't remember, asked for a ride again. "It's OK, everyone
has problems," the leader of the meeting said. And then a few years ago
I was out with Roger having a beer, watching a game
at Carson's Bar & Grill, when a friend of his came in and ducked back out
when he saw us. Roger couldn't make any sense of it. They
were friends, he said. And the guy was going through a
tough time. Why wouldn't he return Roger's calls? Why
withdraw like this? And then a year or so later, Roger got his
terminal prognosis and stopped returning my calls. I
had to find out he left town by seeing his car gone.

So when I look out at the world and am humbled
by all the ways the trees and rivers

pass our understanding, I can maybe take a bit of solace
in the fact that we do a pretty good job passing our understanding
as well. Still, we have the houses and buildings, the trees
and train schedules. It's not nothing. As you have to try
to understand the things you cannot destroy.

LXIII

Why not love pictures? Each time they come back,
they come back in exactly the same way, and sometimes
quite unexpectedly from a box. What's not
to love about that? And then the ones that are unattributed,
like the ones Rosie brought in once
from a trunk she found in the basement
of her duplex. Two women in the 1940s or maybe early 50s
in front of a tract home, and the younger one, pretty
with dark hair and dark lips, looking at the camera
with a "please hurry up and get me out of here" look,
so that forever she'll be wanting to get out from this place
she's certainly gotten out of by now.

And still she gets to be pretty, and the shot, a little
square, gets to be pretty as well, with the scalloped
edges. The way memory is mostly collective, as we practice it
in front of people who tell it back to us
or have it place itself around these pictures, and my baby
pictures as well, inscribed with someone's handwriting I've never met,
"Marty 11 mos." So I got to be a Marty for a few years.
I remember it the way I can feel sometimes that I remember
being on the moon, my feet in the baby powder of it, the flag
with the wire top that doesn't blow.

The other day I saw a picture of the band
I used to be in twenty years ago,
and remembered we played a strip club by accident once,
a few days before it was taken,
as our drummer knew a drummer who said we could play this club,
see, without telling us what kind of club it was, so
there I was singing Neil Young's "Hey Hey, My My (Into the Black)"
while a mostly naked woman danced beside me
around a pole. I'm glad there are no pictures of that moment,
as all of us seemed to be on a race
to find who could be the most not there.

LXIV

When one studies math, they say that what's important
is not the algorithm per se, but the logic
behind it. It's never what it is. Or it's always what it is
but what it is isn't what one might be thinking
it is. Like being useful, how there are many ways
to be useful that aren't about carrying boxes. Mark
wrote to tell me that in deeper ways I probably am, and have been, useful
to many persons. "Probably mainly in good ways," he said,
"though there is also the possibility of having been useful to someone
in a bad way (as when we speak of having been used
by someone)." And how, then, that might have even turned out
to be useful, who knows. I have this vision of myself
bumbling through my life, suddenly, in a sort of "Pippa Passes" way,
where all manner of good befalls the people I accidentally cut off
on the freeway. I just looked up "Pippa Passes" and found
it's not just the drama by Browning, but also the name of a city
in Knott County, Kentucky, where possibly a lot of good luck resides.
What bad relationship have I been in that I can possibly
test this out on? Maybe we could make a few calls, ask about my
cruelties and the cruelties done to me. Sit
and think awhile. I suppose the worst thing I can think of right now
is how I just found out last spring that the child my first wife said
was mine, and then said wasn't, turns out to have been mine
after all. He's twenty-five now. When he contacted me,
I think he was prepared for me to be hostile
or to try to ignore him. Mostly I was sad. Maybe that's
a kind of being useful, where all we could do was talk.

I wanted a girl to talk to me once when I was twenty-five,
and she wouldn't. I even went by her work, as she was a checkout girl
at the HEB in New Braunfels, Texas. She only looked at me
and rang up my groceries. Maybe that was useful. Maybe
it's all been useful. How a couple years after that, I got fired
from my job at the radio station there, and they took my keys
and escorted me to my car, so I left. And I almost felt important,

knowing they'd have to change the transmitter security codes,
and how I wondered for weeks if they did. So then I went
to graduate school. All useful, how all I have
of my own birth-father is a picture that I ripped in half once
for no reason I can remember. Such things are useful
in the "everything I've been through
has made me who I am today" way, which leads to
people not wanting to take their medications, especially people
with psychological disorders, afraid it will change them. Change. Change.
But mostly, we're not in charge of whether we're useful
to others or not. (Was I? Wasn't I?) Maybe "useful" isn't
a good enough word for it. But then "helpful"
isn't much better. That's the kicker. Anyone can come back later
to say some little kindness of mine or yours
saved them or nearly did them in, or that some thoughtlessness—
though they didn't recognize it at the time—saved them . . .
or nearly did them in. As in lifting that box, or donating blood,
or that card, or telling them to go fuck themselves. Our
cruelties, followed by some sketchy philosophy.

But still, who's to say? It all becomes part of the mix, so that
however you're doing right now redefines everything
you've been through. The guy that picked me up in his white Econoline van
when I was hitchhiking, who tried to get me to take my
clothes off, and who was a lot bigger that I was,
now, looking around, I guess he helped make me who I am. I got a chance
to practice looking calm and figuring a way out—which,
that time, consisted of me saying how great that sounded,
but that my dorm roommate would, I'm sure, like to join us,
so let me go in and get him, and of course
never coming back. Ian Hunter sings, "I ain't no chain,
I'm just a link . . ." as a sort of mathematics of accretion,
though there's also subtraction and the continuing question
whether math was invented or discovered.
So there at the end, what's the suicide to say
other than everything's all been bad, when it becomes too much,
though obviously everything's not always been bad, or all cruel, so that,
climbing the bridge rigging, say, preparing to throw herself

into the parking lot, we know she's going through something internal
more than external. What's the difference, though, when all we have
is ourselves? There's the river below. It's night. It's
1983, and I'm trying not to panic, and then it's 2009, and in the paper
a woman is looking down from the high wire, filling me
with that fear I get in high places, that I could just step into the air.

LXV

Tonight's program is Clandestinophilia, insisting
we make cookies. It's LXV, the retirement-age. And here I am
nearly a year after first writing this sequence, tossing something in,
as the poem that was here has been merged with LXIV ("Sixty-four
and there's so much more" as Neil Young says.). The lake
continues to ripple. The solar system runs over us
and we take no notice. Time may well be a hallucination, I just read
in *Scientific American*, but if so, the question is why then
is it such a persistent hallucination? My uncle survived the air crash,
though his recovery continues. Mark died. Terri had everyone over
a few weeks after, and we had a nice time. I played his guitar.

You never know what you're going to find. Once, when I was
delivering newspapers, a guy flagged me down,
and then dove into the car through the passenger side window,
finding, when he did, that the car was full of newspapers. He
was terribly drunk, demanding I drive him to the hospital,
as he practically swam around inside my car, so I did. The only other time
someone's done something like that was a few days ago
in Puerto Rico, when a guy jumped on the trunk, directing us through
a tight tunnel to where we could park for "seven dollars
and whatever else you want to add for tip." We thought for a moment
he was leading us to some sort of robbery, it was all so odd. Turns out
we parked in a graveyard at the outskirts of the Castillo de San Felipe
del Morro, at the edge of a cliff overlooking the ocean.

They keep saying Social Security won't be there when I
get to retirement age, and they say this while I continue
to pay into it. I suppose we're all supposed to die young. That would
solve things. I thought I was going to die, briefly,
when I was in the floodwater in Texas twenty years ago, and then again
a few years ago when I went in for the MRI, and I probably looked
like I was capable of killing someone
the time my alternator adjustment rod broke at 4:00 a.m.
while I was on the paper route, and I wedged it back up

with an axe I just happened to have in my trunk. The way I looked
driving down the roads of San Marcos, swerving back and forth,
throwing newspapers out the windows, the axe jutting from under the hood,
the head off to the side like a flag that means you harm.

LXVI

On the airline, I sat next to the woman with the young child,
because I have young children. "Children exist all around us,
through us, beyond us," as the magazine I'm reading says. When I
was six, the child next door drowned in their swimming pool.
He was two. The coffin was the size of a suitcase. We're all
characters in the movie, and the movie is called, "Children Are
the Only Ones Who Exist." According to DNA, that's the meaning
of life. I'm now, in January, on my birthday, the 6th (the Feast
of the Epiphany!), rereading this again. I talk about this
a lot. The tiny coffin. How we got out of school to go. It's
2013 now. The funeral was my first. Forty-two years ago, in Orange
County, California. 1971. Our street was Caltech Circle.
A California technical circle. I watched our neighbor
hammering something in his garage months later, watching
the hammer strike, and the delay, and then the sound.

The error creeps in. The minor flaw gets amplified through
repetition until it comes to characterize the system. "Evolution will make
a mess out of you," as Jay Farrar has it, on "Phosphate Skin." I had
this thought and then I start thinking about some terrible future.
The other night Eliot was playing in our big suitcase. Crouching
and then jumping out. I'm sorry. I have this vision that they're fragile,
my children, usually when one gets sick, which is usually Eliot
first, or I read something in the paper, with an ambulance parked
next door and then leaving slowly, without its siren. But right now
no one's sick. Let's go for a stroll. The clean lines of a room.
Natalie asks for help with her homework. No one's sick. It's OK.

Not so for a waiter I knew when I was a teenager bussing tables
at The Blue Dolphin, Farmingdale, Long Island. There was a bullet hole
in the wall above the bar from when someone was mad at the owner once
(our story was it was the mob), though all it seemed the owner ever did
was smoke cigarettes and eat salad. But the waiter, who I keep going back
to, had an epiphany when he was thirteen, and then somehow
forgot it. "It's all meaningless now," he said to me one night, but I never did

get it. That night he jumped up on the catering tables and danced. He danced like the world was made of fire. He danced like dancing was how one remembers important things.

LXVII

Is there anything that isn't hit or miss? After the believing game
comes the doubting game. There's an unstoppability
to it. And then a "Why the hell should I care about your maundering?"
We want a finishedness to things, except for ourselves, of course.
It's best if we continue unabated as long as there is, passing a lot of places
where, in the past, people defended themselves against other people,
and the elements. Right now, The Flaming Lips are on,
and singing, "I asked you a question. I didn't need you to reply."
The story continues in both directions, forward and back:

One of us, my brother or me, was born in Gresham, Oregon,
and the other in Troutdale. We were born two days apart. I was
on the 6th of January, and he was on the 8th. His mother
was the sister of my father, until years later, when we were adopted
and became brothers. Our mother now, back then, was the daughter
of the brother of my birth grandmother. We scratch our heads about it
now and then, how every family has these stories, these little shufflings,
somewhere. They give us something to talk about, research
opportunities, the occasional father we never knew. But even things
that bother one can't bother one all the time. We get tired. We yearn
for connection, like how I'm yearning now for some reason,
and mostly it's just people sitting there, which is enough, often.
"Learn to Accept Uncertainty," the magazine in front of me goes,
or perhaps one doesn't, right? For the rest of the day
I'll say only things I mean. I'll call people and tell them I love them,
but maybe I'll wear a fake mustache, and no one will know.
Maybe I'll cross my fingers. Some go at silence.

I went to a poetry reading in North Carolina last month, and met a guy
named David, I believe, who was upset about my mention
of John Cage. "He was wrong about silence," he said. "Could be,"
I replied, thinking that being right or wrong about silence is outside
the question of silence. But then again, maybe not. Perhaps
there is someone out there who is right about silence,
which is, as they say, the secret language the dead share with God.

LXVIII

There's always a point at which each of us says
I no longer know the answer. Wittgenstein's famous
passing over in silence moment, hanging there like a carnival.
There's a place where we're always eight years old, like my daughter,
Natalie, standing here, and each word a possible real state
of events. Each question a part of something real
that's missing. Here we are in the window looking out
at the moon. It's full right now, or close enough,
December 1st, 2009. A sort of ethics, looking out.

I've been away from thinking about the landscape
for a week. We soon become distracted, lose the thread,
and begin to think of other things. K has lunch
with her ex, and he's suddenly everything he should have been
when they were together, but wasn't. I read once
that the Son of Sam sometimes would go out with his gun and all,
and not kill anyone. He'd get all ready and then not do it.
And he liked that, he'd say. And this week we got word
that my cousin Bill, who's been a pilot for close to forty years now,
was in a plane crash at takeoff. It was a cargo plane, with
seven crew members on board. Three died, four lived.
He was one of the ones who lived, and he's just been upgraded
from critical to serious. He'll be a long time recovering. They're
already talking about his "new normal." The new thing, the way
Coke was replaced by New Coke. And how that turned out.

When I was four, Bill and his brother Jim would hold my arms
and make me hit myself, saying to me, "Why are you
hitting yourself?" while I was laughing and having
a great time. I knew they were on my side, so it was OK. I told
Natalie and Eliot about that the other night, and held their arms,
made them hit themselves, while asking them, "Why are you
hitting yourself?" That night, at 4:00 a.m., Natalie woke
and called out, "Daddy, I need you." When I got to her room,
she was sitting up in her bed. She turned to me
and asked, "Why do I sing?"

114

LXIX

The new thing. There's always got to be one, because
there are always new people and there has to be something
for them to do. They're always finding things out, even if
others have found them out before. So here I am
wanting to add something else to this poem a year later. It
used to end on LXVIII, but that didn't seem like an ending,
so I added the section that is now LXX, so I need a LXIX,
which is, of course, a funny thing to say when you say it out loud
and people overhear just that last bit. So there we are,
and the question is: do I have something new to say?

Roger left town last week, for good, I guess. He got sick.
A blood disorder, he said, and he just decided to dump the whole
place and head West. Go West! Portland, I hear. He didn't answer
when I called (and I called several times), but I heard from Richard,
who asked him if he was heading off to greener pastures, and he
replied, "Any pastures at all." It's almost a Hollywood ending,
and also charmingly ironic, thinking about this as I'm sitting here
surrounded by bright green pastureland. Well, I had this other idea
just now, that no matter what happens, whatever kind of ending
you get, you always have yourself. In the way that Terri
has herself after Mark died, and the way that Brenda has herself
after the cancer receded. But sometimes I think maybe you don't
even get that. That you might lose track or lose interest
and just wander off in Act III, forgetting all about the apples
and the aerodynamics of fossil birds. Even so, we drove by Roger's
place last week, and he was having a garage sale. No matter
what else happens, dying or not, you still have to do something
with your things. And now, another year later (2011), I've
gotten word that he died yesterday, in Portland, in hospice.

How's that song go, I want to ask him right now, this very
second, but I'm thinking of a song that hasn't been written yet,
called "The World Ends When You Die." It has a simple
chord progression, resolving to the tonic, and it'll be about

duration, and how it's OK not to know what happened. To never know. To drop everything or keep everything, it doesn't matter. *New* is the fantasy. Knowing is beside the point. But still, I wish I knew. I really wish I knew.

LXX

What does a person need, finally? What, specifically,
do I need, beside water, air, and food? "I have this
and need nothing else." Or, as Thom Yorke has it, "I'm
an animal / trapped in your hot car // . . . I only stick with you /
because there are no others." This morning I'm sitting in my pickup
in front of the gym, drinking my coffee. My door's open
in the present tense. (And now there's a second now,
two hours later typing this up.) And I have this feeling
of complete happiness. I know where everyone is,
and everyone's OK. A song is playing on the radio,
"Exhaustible," by DeVotchKa, that I like. There's this part
where a chorus whistles—it just came around again—
that's going well with the light wind and people going by.

When I was a teenager, I read a story about a man
who made a deal with the Devil. The Devil gave him a watch
he could use to stop time when he was completely
happy—the Devil knows human nature, right? No one
knows you better. So the guy's unable to ever hit
the stop button. All his life, through kids
and lovers and success and failure . . . and so then he dies
and finds himself on the hell-bound train,
and the Devil comes for his watch and the guy's soul.

We're always happiest between things: the rush, the
whoosh, the empty space, the impossible
to estimate. I think so, at least, right now, two years
after writing this book, slipping in something new
because I don't want it to be over. So, yes, the guy
pushes the button right there on the train, as I
should be pushing the button right now, I guess, only
there's no button. It's another of the ways
art tricks us, how we might think there's a most
happy. There are some kids practicing soccer
in the field behind the gym, by the water tower.

And "happy" isn't the right word. The right word
is "Landscape," or "I feel I'm on a train."

LXXI

Kings, they say, need reminding, but I don't think so, at least
no more reminding than we all do. How the road forks up ahead, yes,
but it forks behind as well, and all directions are directions
owing more to the weather than what we brought with us. One time,
for instance, I was a boy scout, and we went hiking once a month,
it seemed. On one of the hikes I found a good, strong branch,
and began whittling it into a walking stick. It was so straight. Halfway through,
I lost track of it, and found that another boy had picked it up and whittled it
some more, claiming it. He was so proud of that walking stick,
and he cried when he lost it down a sink hole. I'd already lost it by that time,
so losing sight of it down that hole thrilled me. It was one of my
last hikes. It was in Alabama, and the boy scout troop
flew a Dixie flag, saying it was heritage, not hate. I asked one of them once
if they had a British flag somewhere as well. I liked hiking,
looking at the trees whose names I can never keep straight
in my mind. I get the same feeling walking around town sometimes.

Today, I saw a fox on Sixteenth Street. My five-year-old son, Eliot,
was with me. He said some foxes are big and some are small. And we all
have to live together here. Even if Plato, in a semi-surprising move,
banished poets from the ideal society in Book X of *The Republic*, in which
art cannot be evaluated apart from either its social or political implications,
but mostly artists say, "I'm all out of truth, sorry, but I've plenty
of dare left." It's all a part of my inner calmness. My daughter, Natalie,
who's nine now, working on her inner calmness, gave me some
advice yesterday, saying when Eliot begins to parrot back everything
she says, she's found that saying to him "I'm weird" hoping he'll parrot that
back, runs the risk of having him suddenly break from parroting her first,
and saying back, "yes you are." She's working on a new strategy now,
and she says she'll get back to me on it later. But do we ever get a new strategy,
really? Don't we mostly just count off a string of monuments
or perhaps moments or vice versa, while the ones who will be remembered
are busy in the other room naming buildings after each other?

And that we can always be right in saying "times are tough right now"
because there's always some way we're right, the way a Medicine Man can always
claim success whether it rains or not, and that even the angels
are having to take a bus to heaven these days. And heaven is 7% smaller now,
and has had to cut a couple whole departments. So we ask ourselves
what's left there, and we don't know. But we start off anyway,
because that's what we do. And then one day we just stop.

ℰℐ

ACKNOWLEDGMENTS

Thank you to the editors of the following journals for publishing sections of this poem:

The Academy of American Poets: IV
The Ampersand Review: XV, XV, XVII, XXVI, XXXV
Anti-: XVIII, XIX
At Length: LVII, LVIII, LLIX, LX, LX1, LXII, LXIII, LXIV, LXV
The Awl: XXXVII, XXXVIII
The Bakery: XLIX, L, LI, LII
Better: XLII
BOR: XXII, XXIII, XXIV
The Boston Review Online: XLIII, XLIV
Crazyhorse: XXX, XXIV
Diode: XLVI, XLVII, XLVIII, LXVI
Field: XIII, XV
Fifth Wednesday: XX, XXI
Georgetown Review: V
Hotel Amerika: XXVIII, XXXI, XXXIII, LXX1
Interim: VII, VIII, IX, X, XI, LXVIII
The Kenyon Review: XII
The Literary Review: XXXVI, XL
MAP Literary: LV, LVI
The Massachusetts Review: LXIX
The New England Review: VI
Omniverse: LXVII, LXX
The Ostrich Review: XXV, XXXII
Pinwheel: XXVII, XXIX
Pleiades: XLI
Poetry: I, II, III
The Southeast Review: XLV
West Branch: LIII, LIV

Special thanks to G.C. Waldrep, Dana Levin, and David Dodd Lee for invaluable assistance and support, and to Armin Mühsam, for his drawings and his friendship. Thank you to Peter Conners and everyone at BOA for taking a chance.

For Natalie, Eliot, and Robin

> Take the case of a man for whom reality is enough, as, at the end
> of his life, he returns to it like a man returning from Nowhere
> to his village and to everything there that is tangible and visible
> which he has come to cherish and wants to be near.
>
> —Wallace Stevens, *Collected Poetry & Prose*

This poem was written while listening to an album of John Cage compositions titled *In a Landscape*, Stephen Drury, piano, while also reading Cage's *SILENCE*. Some of the language and imagery (and tone) of this poem owes itself to those works.

About the Author

John Gallaher is the author of *The Little Book of Guesses* (2007, Four Way Books), winner of the Levis Poetry prize; *Map of the Folded World* (2009, University of Akron Press); and co-author, with G.C. Waldrep, of *Your Father on the Train of Ghosts* (2011, BOA Editions), as well as co-editor of *Time Is a Toy: The Selected Poems of Michael Benedikt* (2014, University of Akron Press). His poetry appears widely in such places as *The Boston Review, Crazyhorse, Field, The Kenyon Review, Poetry,* and *Pleiades,* and in anthologies including *The Best American Poetry.* Gallaher is currently associate professor of English at Northwest Missouri State University, and co-editor of *The Laurel Review,* and The Akron Series in Poetics.

BOA Editions, Ltd. American Poets Continuum Series

COLOPHON

BOA Editions, Ltd., a not-for-profit publisher of poetry and other literary works, fosters readership and appreciation of contemporary literature. By identifying, cultivating, and publishing both new and established poets and selecting authors of unique literary talent, BOA brings high-quality literature to the public. Support for this effort comes from the sale of its publications, grant funding, and private donations.

❧

The publication of this book is made possible, in part,
by the special support of the following individuals:

Anonymous x 3
Kazim Ali & Marco Wilkinson
Armbruster Family Foundation
Wyn Cooper
Susan DeWitt Davie
Jonathan Everitt
Suzanne Gouvernet
Michael Hall
The Henschel/Piccione Family, *in loving memory of Jarret Lobb*
X. J. & Dorothy M. Kennedy
Barbara & John Lovenheim
Chandra V. McKenzie
Daniel M. Meyers
Boo Poulin
Deborah Ronnen & Sherman Levey
Steven O. Russell & Phyllis Rifkin-Russell
David W. Ryon

Printed in the USA
CPSIA information can be obtained
at www.ICGtesting.com
JSHW062003090124
55097JS00008B/23

9 781938 160509